TIMING
THINK
THINKING
TIME

A BEGINNER'S
CRITICAL HISTORICAL
SOCIOLOGY REDUX

VIRGILIO ROJAS

Third Eye Publishers

ISBN: 1492858706
ISBN: 978-1492858706

Cover image courtesy of thejonk.tictail.com

DEDICATION

To the memory of my brothers, Augusto and Gilberto Rojas, who have recently departed and ascended to Higher Light.

CONTENTS

ACKNOWLEDGMENTS

Professor Ulf Jonsson, my dissertation supervisor at the Department of Economic History at Stockholm University, deserves credit for the initial push generating the shove that brought this text to its conclusion.

A similar notification of inspirational debt goes to the late Professor Charles Tilly and his lecture on recent works in Comparative Historical Sociology I attended at the Higher Seminar sponsored and organized by the Department in the late 90s. His wit, candor and advocacy of academic transparency added spice to the broth of this book.

And finally, to my friend Jon Knutsson alias TheJonk, the creator of this book's cover image, a warm embrace for sharing his heart and inimitable art.

PREFACE

Timing Think, Thinking Time is second in a series of four Vintage Debate Reloads "cinematographically" reproducing, i.e., incorruptibly replaying in its entirety, the author's critical review of some of the most significant contemporary theoretical disputes in the post-structural, post-colonial, post-modern late 80s to the 90s. These reproductions are verbatim as it were, without revision of the original texts, and rather intentionally retaining all the idiomatic expressions and conceptual furniture associated with classic debates around themes as varied as Marxism in post-colonial societies like the Philippines; Gender in the history of European labor; Latin American economies and the relativity of dependency theory; Thinking time and timing think in Historical Sociology; Urban History; Collective Action and Alienation.

By resurrecting these texts, the food for thought the author hopes to raise in the mind of today's global reader is the impermanence of monologic narratives and the permanence of dialogic movements—in the sense of Eugene Irschick (1994) recycling M. Bakhtin's concept (2002)—whether by design or default, in the history and evolution of paradigms and scientific discourses. Any prolonged attempt to mainstream any thought, any protracted attempt to ensconce and transform any thought into a monologue, will always provoke countervailing attempts toward nuancing, critical dialogue, and eventually, the assertion of dialogic transactions of thought, later, and inevitably, the amnesia that often follows in terms of the existence of such transactions over time. The aim here is simply to remind all of us that those transactions should not be forgotten and that every monologic narrative today will breed its dialogic alter ego at any other point in time.

Critical dialogue in this book is traced by the classic metaphor of *modernity/modernization* and was originally supposed to be transacted within a single-frame narrative. Within this main frame, the design frame if you like, I, as a graduate student in the mid-90s, was required and expected to hone standard skills in the art of critical scientific writing according to the endorsed rules of rational economy, efficiency, elegance and exactitude. Yet, as I, pursuing the role of dispassionate observer, negotiated what was after all a

simulated dialogue among a handful of peer-selected writers according to those terms, I felt and would soon discover that obsequious compliance with the rules of the game didn't necessarily add up to the methodological transparency and rigor I believed they were ultimately designed to serve.

Concern for the issue of transparency, made the process of refining the prose of this book from my raw if systematic forensic notes writhe agonizingly between the choice of streamlining the text by the sanctioned standards of design and that of defaulting or not relinquishing on/to those standards by retaining significant segments of the raw text.

Oscillations of this nature in the context of scientific narrative construction portray how dialogic transactions co-exist and co-extend even within what may at first sight appear to be a singular process, a singular narrative. Moreover, some of them, like the one noted here, are often transacted in the fine-print, taken for granted and at best acknowledged only parenthetically, but rarely told outside the silent realm of the backstage unless fully and finally rehearsed in their most refined, revered articulations, that of the scientific article or monograph.

Ultimately, as I decided to go for more of the standard deviation and the rawer version, my examiner/advisor, while validating my work, expectedly suggested to default less, rationalize (in the Swedish sense of *rationalisera* or streamlining) and deflate the text henceforth. Honestly, though, I am glad for not having second-guessed my gut-felt choice of disobedience by both allowing noted otherwise submerged narrative to emerge and confronting the aesthetics of academic refinement with that of its raw alter ego, without which this book would have hardly been anticipated.

1

INTRODUCTION

COMPARATIVE HISTORICAL SOCIOLOGY —PROJECT, PROSPECTS & PROBLEMS OF 'BIG THINK' & 'BIG TIME'

While foraging through the special course list for additional units, I came across a newly entered course in Historical Sociology, which immediately attracted my attention. Rather than novelty, what mainly attracted me I guess was the duality of identity it evoked. Intuitively, the title suggested synthesis or some sort of unifying intellectual program for what would traditionally be perceived as disciplinary paired-opposites with well-guarded boundaries—*History*, dedicated to contingency, agency and singular events, and, *Sociology*, committed to theory, structures and causality.

Again, intuitively, just as with other similar unifying crusades, I could imagine historical sociologists stirring up a hornets nest of critics from respective parental guiders, but also encountering problems indigenous to synthesizing enterprise itself, and certain neurotic twists which might stem from the duality of identity itself. Excitedly, I decided to take the course and find out if my hunch served me right.

At the outset, the question of identity poses itself automatically. What is *Historical Sociology*? What precisely sets it apart from its genetic parents, History and Sociology? What might be the key features of this purportedly integrated research program and strategy? Why not settle for the time-tested technologies already there in either one of the two disciplines? And why stake your bet on Historical Sociology at all?

In a classic manifesto, Abrams (1982)[1] tells us why "a single unified program of analysis"[2] is in order. He states the case somewhat psychologically by pointing at subliminal and often repressed cross-tendencies hidden in the works of historians and sociologists alike, which neither of them are often aware of, nor would wish to admit. That is, there are historical presuppositions concealed within Sociology as much as there are sociological presuppositions hidden within historical works.[3] These cross-tendencies exist to the extent that History and Sociology share the problem cluster of 'structuring' as a relation between action and structure. "Far from speaking for itself," Abrams contends, "the reality of the past speaks only when first firmly spoken to by the historian." And therefore, one should superimpose "structure on history with a view to

---

[1]*Historical Sociology*. London: Open Books.

[2]quoted in Smith, Dennis (1991) *The Rise of Historical Sociology*. Cambridge: Polity Press. (p. 3)

[3]Leca has argued in partial defense of Abrams' vision in this manner. Leca, Jean (1992) "Postface: Has Historical Sociology Gone Back to its Infancy? Or When Sociology Gave Up to History," *ISSJ* 133: 403-415.

recovering the way history superimposes structure on us."[4]

Historical Sociology would provide effective therapeutic means to tease out these hidden tendencies by 'submitting history' not to what Abrams labeled "the a-historical fetishism of (sociological) theory as knowledge, but by offering to those historians engaged in work of singular narration(s) the means to guard themselves against "the anti-theoretical fetishism of history-as-evidence."[5]

A less dramatic and more lexical answer to noted questions can be found in the more recent formulation of Dennis Smith (1991).[6]

> "Historical Sociology is the study of the past to find out how societies work and change. Some sociologists are 'non-historical': empirically, they neglect the past; conceptually, they consider neither the time dimension of social life, nor the historicity of social structure. Similarly, some historians are 'non-sociological': empirically, they neglect the way processes and structures vary between societies; conceptually, they consider neither the general properties of processes and structures, nor their relationships to acts and events. By contrast historical sociology is carried out by historians and sociologists who investigate the mutual interpenetration of past and present, events and processes, acting and structuration. They try to marry *conceptual clarification, comparative generalization, and empirical exploration*." (emphasis mine)

The core vision and principles proposed by both Abrams and

---

[4]Abrams cited in McMichael, Philip (1992) "Rethinking Comparative Analysis in a Post-Development Context," *ISSJ* 133: 351-366.

[5]Abrams quoted in Leca, *op cit.*

[6]Smith, *op cit.*: 3.

Smith take their hitherto most modular expression in Theda Skocpol's (1984) celebrated attempt to set the formal rules for sound and 'truly historical sociological studies' and to define operational procedures for the craft, preferably, towards causality-seeking 'analytic' research directions. She sorts out authentic from defective Historical Sociology among the wide variety of works available according to four key quality-controlling precepts, some or all of which must be satisfied.

Thus the work x rises to the occasion if x: 1) asks questions about social structures or processes concretely situated in time and space; 2) addresses processes over time and takes temporal sequences seriously in accounting for outcomes; 3) considers the interplay of meaningful action and structural contexts to grasp both intended and unintended outcomes in individual lives and social transformations; 4) highlights the particular and varying features of particular social structures and patterns of changes.[7]

While Skocpol's game-rules optimize in principle the task of bringing 'theory and history' to bear on one another, in practice, she singles out the analysis of causal regularities in history as being so far the best of three available research strategies (*cf* applying either general models to or concepts for reinterpreting history) for guaranteeing maximum results.

Cutting out the odd edges from above accounts, noted trio do broadly bond within a homogenizing discourse in favor of a unifying program—with Abrams telling us why it is strategically compelling to do so, with Smith further clarifying the concrete implications of such a program, and with Skocpol providing the ground rules for introducing disciplinary order into an otherwise fractious market of existing

---

[7]Skocpol, Theda (1984) *Vision and Method in Historical Sociology*. New York: CUP. pp- 1 *ff*, 356 *ff*.

Historical Sociologies and the standard most effective means or method by which to achieve unification.

Against their kindred optimism there is the sobering skepticism of Charles Tilly. Ironically, this writer, while currently ranked as one of the most innovative masters in the trade of disciplinary synthesis even by Skocpol's rigorous standards, has also been one of the leading advocates of preserving the relative autonomy of the two disciplines. The institutionalization of Historical Sociology, he argues, may very well impede the spread of historical thinking to other parts of Sociology. Tilly's skepticism anticipates crucial methodological tensions associated with the art of synthesis to be elaborated further on here, and is couched in terms which in an amusing way inverts Abram's psychological justification for unification by alluding to what Guy Hermet[8] dubbed as the 'repressed historian' complex afflicting many historical sociologists today:[9]

> "There is a great danger there that too few (sociologists) will push beyond the collation of published historical accounts to the systematic analysis of primary historical materials, and that sociologists will thereby compound the errors of the historian from whom they draw."

BIG THINK, BIG TIME & COMPARISON

Reloading our original question on identity, at least three outstanding elements can be extracted from these motley depositions, as far as basic trademarks and twists of the craft are concerned. The average fingerprint blotter of Historical Sociology leaves varying impressions of what we may label *big think* and *big time*, often mediated by the method and

---

[8]Hermet, Guy (1992) "On Historical Obstinacy." *ISSJ* 133: 343-350.

[9]Culled from and quoted in Leca, *op cit.*: 403.

technology of comparison. The first two stem logically from the basic thrust of fusing, as earlier noted, History with Sociology. Big think sets its mark on the myriad ways practitioners apply sociological theory and concepts to historical studies, either for purposes of illustration, re-interpretation, theory-testing or causal searching. It means bringing the 'clock-work' of large structures and processes into the otherwise classic singular-event-agenda of many historians.

In the opposite direction, big time refers to making otherwise 'timeless' sociological theories and concepts 'tick,' i.e., examining the diversity and evolution of large structures and processes historically over the long haul, thereby bringing history to bear on the classic a-historical agenda of many sociologists. Technically, in spatial and temporal terms, the thrust of 'making Sociology tick and History run clockwork' almost always operates on the basis of either single or multiple comparisons. Finally, as we shall see later, these features form the Janus-face of Historical Sociology: half of which exudes intellectual inspiration for some, while the other evoking fierce controversy and debate.

With these three features in mind as organizing themes, and exercising some tricks of the trade just learned, this book will first extend the preceding discourse on identity by critically comparing Dennis Smith's (1991) and Theda Skocpol's (1984) somewhat differently designed yet complementary résumés of the state of the art. In Smith's account of the postwar rise of the genre, he develops an argument for a 'Historical Sociology of Historical Sociology,' the conjunctural swings of which are keyed on changes in predominant ideological and political contexts. While this leads him to accentuate similarities and depict craft development in terms of a distinct trajectory, Skocpol contrastingly draws the thread of her survey from methodology(-ies) and the diversity of current research agendas and strategies. As elsewhere noted, her review is intended to beef up normative arguments in support of an analytic macro-causal comparative research strategy.

After appraising the relative utility of Smith and Skocpol's respective 'road maps' over postwar Historical Sociology, we then put rubber on the road by critically juxtaposing the performance records of four practitioners in the art of big think, big time and comparative technology, threshing out strategic prospects and problems incorporated in their respective practices. Here, we will first cross-examine Max Weber's (1986) classic versus Göran Therborn's (1995) modern deployment of comparative historical method to address the time-honored sociological concept of 'modernity,' with the view of bringing out the differences between what this writer perceives as deductive and inductive approaches.

Thereafter, we will counterpoise the paired works of Charles Tilly (1993, 1990), one of the guild's most credible yet controversial masters against Viviana Zelizer's (1994), to highlight the discrepancies between the best of big-time-and-huge/multiple-case-comparative traditions and what may be viewed as the budding new Historical Sociology's more modest application of medium-think-medium-time-network-focused-case-comparative models.

In sundry ways, both also link up with the concept of 'modernity,': with, on the one hand, Tilly tracing how multiple pre-modern state types in Europe via changes in the requirements of war-making eventually did, over the long-run, tread a similar trajectory towards its modern form, and how this process conjoined with the secular development of revolutionary situations and outcomes on the continent, and, on the other, Zelizer historically illuminating over the medium span the process in the United States of the social construction and reconstruction of money, the single most significant medium of expression of Weber's modern rationally calculating economy.

Next, we will diagnose these works' comparative prospects and problems. Scoreboard results will then be connected in the concluding section to the recurring standard design flaws and breakpoints identified by critics of Historical Sociology in the current international debate.[10] Controversy here centers on among others: the application of concepts and macro-sociological comparative procedures to history.

---

[10]The main battle-lines in the debate has been drawn from articles and rejoinders of Bertrand Badie, Charles Tilly, Guy Hermet, Philip MacMichael, SN Eisenstadt and Jean Leca appearing in a special issue on Historical Sociology of *ISSJ*, *op cit*. For further reading see also Kohli A, Evans P, Prezeworski A, Katzenstein P, Scott J and Skocpol T (1995) "The Role of Theory in Comparative Politics: A Symposium." *World Politics* Vol 48 (October): 1-49.

2

TWO ALTERNATIVE
ROAD MAPS

SMITH VERSUS SKOCPOL
BASIC FORMATS, SCOPES AND ARGUMENTS

Before actually engaging the unique contributions of Weber, Therborn, Tilly and Zelizer, a rookie in Historical Sociology like myself would probably first wish to get a quick, overall picture of past and present mainstream currents in the art. Some initial reference points on the art's *differentia specifica* have been served by Abrams and company, but we would like to know more about how mainstream practices have as defined actually evolved since the postwar era, as well as put actual faces on abstract definitions by sorting out who's who among active craft-practitioners.

For these purposes, Smith and Skocpol serve us both with two expedient but differently organized 'road maps'. Our critical comparison of them here will try to evaluate their utility as way-finding tools for the uninitiated beginner.

MAPPING WITH POLITICS AND IDEOLOGY IN COMMAND?

Aside from its wider coverage, what fascinates the beginner in Smith's survey is its creative use of the Historical Sociology approach itself to plot both the development and dynamics of what it calls the 'second long wave' postwar revival of Historical Sociology in the Anglo-Saxon, and to some extent, Francophone, world. Like the preceding first wave—spear-headed by the pioneering works of Marx, Durkheim and Weber on the origins and workings of Western capitalism, crash-landing as it were during the inter-war years—this current wave, is, as argued, driven by an identical need to make sense of contemporary political events. From this vantage point, Smith weaves the red thread of the epic. Thus, he claims that the postwar resurgence of Historical Sociology, and successive phases of its rise may be linked to changes in political conjunctures and characteristic 'moods' among historical sociologists.

Concretely, this translates into two related arguments: a) the question of capitalist democracy's acceptability or viability links the works in all three phases among postwar historical sociologists; 2) political and ideological shifts within Western capitalist democracies and in the latter's external relations have helped shape the problematique of historical sociologists in successive phases. Smith then maps out three major phases, each marked by a distinctive approach to the big think issues of democracy, capitalism, power and values within the 'discipline,' as much as by a varying appreciation and application of both time (History) and comparison.

These phases form the parameters within which Smith at length compares and considers the original contributions of eighteen trend-setters (and a few 'trend-killers,' as it were); or more strictly, thirteen sociologists (Parson, Smelser, Eisenstadt, Bendix, Skocpol, Lipset, Moore, Marshall, Wallerstein, Runciman, Giddens, Mann and Elias), four historians (Thompson, Anderson, Bloch and Braudel), and one odd sociologist-historian (Tilly).[11] Briefly, let's shortcut Smith's schematic to see what distinctively earmarks each phase and whose 'faces' match which phase!

PHASE I (1950s-mid-1960s) In the wake of the Cold War, US style politics and ideology of liberal democracy based on the ideal of strong consensus in a self-evident just order with equal opportunity becomes the leading brand of capitalist democracy in the West. Co-extensively, within Sociology, modernization and structural-functionalist models set the pace and direction of big think enterprise towards expounding how and why capitalist democracy works. Theoretically, the latter is understood to operate as a social system in homeostasis with in-built damage-control and repair capabilities to contain expected and actual imbalances produced by processes of social differentiation between the legitimizing values and perceived interests of specific groups. In this context, Sociological theory takes precedence over History and comparative technology—to the extent the latter were applied, they would serve mainly to prop theory, not to test it. As such, this puts Historical Sociology in a state of strategic defensive. Trend-setters (or trend-killers as far as Historical Sociology is concerned)[12] for this phase were Parsons (1951, 1966, 1971), Smelser (1959), Lipset (1958, 1960, 1963, 1967, 1971) with Eisenstadt (1963) as an odd outlier in this group of structural-functionalists. Trend-breakers[13] and harbingers of the next

---

[11]See Figure 1 in *Appendix*.

[12]In the sense that he focused on pre-industrial empires and not capitalist democracy as such, although he had some relevant comments on the latter. Otherwise, the common denominator among Parson, Smelser and Lipset was the emphasis on the self-adjusting and stabilizing mechanisms inherent in capitalist democracy.

[13]Like Lipset, Marshall saw a conflict between equality through citizenship, and

phase were TH Marshall (1963, 1965, 1969) and Bendix (1964, 1970, 1974, 1978), insofar as both started to shift big think focus away from consensus onto systems-contradictions.

PHASE II (mid-1960s–1970s) Amidst the Vietnam War, rising political militancy of popular movements (anti-colonial, women's civil rights, black, student) and Marxist zeitgeist, the once vaunted full-proof North American and Western model of liberal democracy falls under siege, at which point the intellectual mood switches from justifying to exposing the limits and contradictions of capitalist democracy. In tandem with this political conjuncture, big think within Sociology shifts channels to re-explore issues of domination, inequality and social resistance; taking History more seriously to nail, this time, both the contingencies and regularities of structures and processes, and applying comparative technology for purposes either of theory-testing, historical re-interpretation, or causal analysis. Under these conditions, Historical Sociology breaks out of its previous structural-functionalist straitjacket, shifting in the process from a strategic defensive to a strategic offensive position. Path-breakers[14] like Lenski (1966), Runci-

---

inequality through the market, while the latter was more aware of the disruptive potential of this basic tension. Bendix, drawing from Marshall, argued not only that systems contradictions reduced the efficiency of institutions (e.g., education), but also that value conflicts frequently coincided with lines of group differentiation (e.g., employers versus workers). In other words, societies undergoing industrialization and political modernization did not always handle derived conflicts in ways that lead to stable capitalist democracies.

[14]Lenski and Runciman both dealt with the issue of social stratification as the key source of inequality within societies. Against Parson, Lenski, exploring the role played by power and privilege, argued that societies were imperfect systems with a large measure of coercion and conflict. In the same vein, Runciman asserted that both perceptions about and existing patterns of inequality were in many respects invalid to criteria of social justice. Hence, both undermine the assumption that social order (capitalist democracy) rested on spontaneous acceptance of transparently justifiable norms. As such, they made power and values available as critical concepts, sensitive to coercion and injustice. From

man (1966), Bloch (1961, 1966, 1973) and Elias (1978, 1983) facilitated inter-phase transition for trend-setters[15] like Moore (1969, 1978) and Thompson (1968, 1979).

PHASE III (mid-1970s–1980s) In the same manner as defeat in Vietnam and continued radicalism at home seriously damaged the political legitimacy of US-spun liberal democracy, so did the combined 'Tet offensive' of revisionist and radical critics within Sociology powerfully discredit the legitimacy of structural-functionalist and modernization theory. Rising first to the occasion to fill in the blanks left by the latter's retreat were influential neo/Marxist trend-setters like Wallerstein (1974, 1980) and Anderson (1974), whose works moved previous big think emphasis on the right to the left-hand side of the capitalism-democracy equation. Both sought to explore and expose the provenance and dynamics of capitalism on the basis of comparison designed to do big time (across epochs) and big space (multiple cases and moving scale-unit from national to global). Other more theoretically eclectic practitioners like Skocpol, Tilly, Braudel, Mann and Giddens––whose works served in critical ways to domesticate reductionist tendencies cultivated by the first duo[16]—cohered

---

continental Europe, Bloch and Elias leveled attention at the problem and configuration of power and collective mentalities over time. Neither of them regarded 'integrating values' or political ideologies as a datum handed down by the 'system' as many structural-functionalists tended to assume.

[15]Moore and Thompson demonstrated in different ways the violent nature of capitalist democracy's past, further extending the critique of the latter in succeeding works to argue that modern capitalist democracies were 'predatory' (Moore) or 'parasitical' (Thompson), treating citizens as victims in these relations.

[16]They mitigated against reductionist tendencies most importantly by for example: 1) exploring the active contribution by relatively autonomous state bureaucracies, in their civic and military forms, to the shaping of capitalist economies; 2) treating economic, political and other forms of coercion, each in their own right as relatively independent expressions of power, and without reducing one to the other in theoretical explanations.

in securing and expanding the intellectual territory of Historical Sociology during this phase.

(POST?) PHASE IV (1980s-1990s) Smith adds yet a fourth to the three phases he had exhaustively discussed. This current phase is denoted by a revivalist big think trend back to a re-examination of the right-hand side problem of democracy. Again, as in the other phases, this derived from the logic of contemporary political conjuncture, marked, this time, by the mutual collapse of the politics and ideology of socialist materialism on the left and liberal individualism on the right. In the late 1980s and early 1990s, there were no cut-and-dried alternatives available to resolve the principal issues of the day—abuse of power and rights of citizenship—as the moral force of Marxism had just been shattered by the Soviet experience at the very point when the free-market rhetoric of Margaret Thatcher and Ronald Reagan was losing its self-confidence. Concomitantly, conventional ideological ex-planations, previously deployed to handle problems of power, morality and human experience, had been undermined; Historical Sociology was itself one of the casualties. In this light, a critical re-examination of democracy as a political model has been gaining ground to the extent that Parsonian and Marshallian big think (conflict between class and citizenship) started to attract renewed attention in the late 1980s. However, as Smith asserts, the infrastructure of Historical Sociology still remained quite considerable, and some current practitioners like Simon Schama (1987, 1989) and Paul Kennedy (1987) have generated extensive popularity as international best-sellers.

Beyond the main menu of Historical Sociology's political and ideological dynamics over time, Smith takes us in the concluding part of his road map to a short detour into the Sociology of big think by comparing the varying social and institutional bases and environs in which selected historical sociologists operated.

Ultimately, recalling our introductory quote on Smith (p. 3) about the qualifying features of the art, respective works under review were comparatively ranked according to the degree and extent by which they, implicitly or explicitly, relate to four central elements: primary exploration of specific historical situations, empirical generalizations (i.e., drawing from the explorations of others, referring tacitly or overtly to theoretical issues), systematic theorizing about processes of historical change, and explanatory strategies. Complications and overlaps among sampled writers and works alluded to reappear here with even greater clarity. While these last issues fall more at the margins of Smith's main arguments, they occupy center stage in Skocpol's map, to which we shall now turn.

MAPPING WITH TECHNOLOGY IN COMMAND

In contrast to Smith's comprehensive politics-ideology-based monographic map, Skocpol's concise yet more in-depth mapping of twentieth century Historical Sociology draws from the collective insights of nine current practitioners, each in critical dialogue with one celebrated doyen in the field. At the opposite sides of the discussion table in this anthology, we find Daniel Chirot deliberating with Marc Bloch, Fred Block and Margaret Somers with Karl Polyani, Gary Hamilton with SN Eisenstadt, Dietrich Rueschemeyer with Reinhard Bendix, Mary Fulbrook and Skocpol herself with Perry Anderson, EK Trimberger with EP Thompson, Lynn Hunt with Charles Tilly, Charles Ragin and Chirot once again with Immanuel Wallerstein, and lastly, our previous map designer, Dennis Smith, with Barrington Moore. The thread spun from the minutes of these table conversations and eventually honed as the central argument and format for mapping current state of the art, may be captioned as technology (ies) or methodology (ies) in command!

We shortcut Skocpol this time to bring out the contrast with

Smith. In her version, we find the preceding politics/ideology-dynamized big think shifting over time acknowledged, yet not as central to the drama. Instead, her road map interprets Historical Sociology's ebb and flow more matter-of-factly as part of a "continuing, ever-renewed tradition of research for understanding the nature and effects of large-scale structures and fundamental processes of change."

The logic and object of renewal in the 'master agendas' once set by the pioneers of Historical Sociology like Marx, Durkheim and Weber, stem not so much from the big think questions they posed (i.e., the origins and effects of Western industrial capitalism and democracy)—in essence these issues continue to preoccupy their heirs to date, more or less—as from the distinctive methods deployed by past and present practitioners for bringing sociological theory and historical fact (social structures and events) to bear upon each other.

Departing from the comparative historical method as least common denominator and skeleton key by which to compare old and new research agendas in the art, Skocpol distinguishes and discusses at length three archetypal applications of standard technology and their respective ramifications on the central task of mediation noted above.

Thus, albeit leaving space for possible overlaps and 'creative' combinations, historical sociologists may be ranked according to whether they: 1) apply a general model to explain historical instances; 2) use concepts to develop meaningful historical interpretations; or 3) analyze causal regularities in history. After assaying the pros and cons of each on the basis of a few case illustrations, Skocpol then singles out and recommends the third model as the ultimate, most effective means by which to obtain the best possible fusion between theory and history.

As advertised before, strategy 3 (analytic) overrides the first two alternatives as best brand choice. Unlike strategy 2 (interpretative) employing comparative technology to mainly demonstrate historical variation, this approach uses such technology to bring out both differences and similarities, examining historical variations to establish causal regularities and develop adequate explanations. Contrary to strategy 1 (straight model application), it does not make historical cases merely accountable to any given theoretical model a priori, but rather engage comparative evidence to test the validity of alternative hypotheses and explanatory arguments.

While the latter may be derived either deductively from two or more pre-existing theories, or inductively by 'causally significant analogies between instances' during the course of investigation, the crucial point for strategy 3 is that no effort is made to analyze historical fact according to a preconceived model. Research always addresses a clearly posed historical question here. This is a defining point for feeding the diverse agendas of Polanyi, Bloch, Moore, Tilly (and Skocpol herself) into a single third strategy box.

Hypothesis-testing agendas are also far more inclined towards multiple rather than single case comparisons than the two other alternatives.[17] Within this third strategy, either one of two basic tactics, exclusively or inclusively, define comparative operations among different practitioners; what with John Stuart Mills, Skocpol designates as the method of agreement (MoA) versus the method of difference (MoD).

Simply put, MoA tactics 'positively' juxtapose cases, which, while apparently differing in salient respects, substantially

---

[17]Comparative historical analysis as Skocpol points out however contrasts to probabilistic technics of statistical analysis in that it proceeds through logical juxtapositions of aspects of a small number of cases and attempts to identify invariant causal configurations that necessarily rather than probably combine to account for outcomes of interest.

share both hypothesized causal factors and the phenomenon or outcome to be explained. MoD tactics contrast and control-check 'positive' against 'negative' cases, which, while sharing salient similarities with the former, essentially neither contain identified causal prerequisites, nor generated the phenomenon or outcome to be explained.

Between the two, Skocpol argues that the second method is most powerful, although combinations may at times be possible and motivated. Her map ends with a footnote on some of analytic Historical Sociology's critical pitfalls and limits, but concludes that strategy 3 after all comparably still constitutes the single most cost-effective technology available for extracting the highest possible returns on any theory-history-comparative-merger-based research project.

APPRAISING ROAD MAP UTILITY AND LIMITS: POLITICS AND IDEOLOGY OR TECHNOLOGY IN COMMAND?

Before making the final score, this Historical Sociology (HS) rookie pauses for a quick cost-benefit estimate of the two road maps on sale, in terms of their functional utility and limits. As noted in the shopping prelims, both draw the career history of Western postwar HS, yet contrast not only in quantitative coverage, but most significantly in cognitive design and normative content.

A beginner who wishes to familiarize with as many of HS craft-masters as possible, as well as access encyclopedic descriptions of their respective chefs d'oeuvre, or one who covets the luxury of situating these works in convenient chronological order over time, will certainly find Smith's map attractive. With the larger context of Western capitalist politics and ideology as organizing legend to account for shifting intellectual 'moods' within HS, he is able to pigeonhole the works of thirteen reputed historical sociologists respectively in three or four more or less coherent phases.

By virtue of this legend, Smith is thus able to portray HS fashion swings, as indicated by what particular big think issues predominate current HS agendas in consecutive phases, according to the three-phase trajectory metaphor of 'phoenix rising from the ashes' (i.e., the prohibitive sway of a-historical structural functionalism in the 1950s), 'taking flight' (in the 1960s and 1970s), and 'soaring high' (in the 1970s and 1980s, and apparently, although Smith refrains from extending the metaphor, 'maintaining altitude' in the 1980s and beyond).

Indeed, Smith's map has the makings of a well-scripted narrative of, as he described it himself, the 'Historical Sociology of Historical Sociology.' Unlike Skocpol's, his enticing narrative avoids the controversy of prescription, restraining map utility largely to the comparative and descriptive. In other words, while he does thresh out significant similarities and dissimilarities among current agendas, he leaves the prerogative of evaluating their respective use-values entirely to the map reader.

However, the advantage of this map has its critical flip-side. Firstly, while defining and comparing both HS phases and matching 'faces' or works prominently on the basis of current big think issues posed clearly, indeed even graphically, do bring out both commonalities within and contrasts between identified phases, it, at the same time, fogs other equally significant commonalities across and contrasts within respective phases, which could very well have made for interesting comparison. Secondly, granting for the sake of argument that the latter is the price Smith pays for coherence, his account tends at times to perhaps be too coherent that it raises reasonable suspicion. Counterpoising Skocpol to him as such, one notes that beyond the veneer of big think issues, the boundaries between Smith's phases do quiver and overlap on several dimensions. At these points, his map surrenders with suspicious levity coherence to clarity: theoretical and methodological genealogies connecting writers across phases with the legacies of celebrated HS pioneers like Weber, Durkheim and Marx are inadequately accounted for.

While accounting for changes in mainstream HS issues are not insignificant, Skocpol argues that in fact, insofar as current HS agendas recap essentially veteran issues of capitalism and democracy once posed by the pioneers, these discrepancies may very well be nominal and that mapping concerns should instead be directed to the varying and kindred ways in which past and current HS addresses these questions through comparative historical technology.

In this sense, Skocpol's map—navigating along technology or methodological lines rather than issues (i.e., the modes by which writers confront theory with history), supplemented by a clearer account on theoretical linkages—is able to turn Smith's critical weakness to its own advantage.

Using method as organizing legend enables her to substitute the coherence of Smith's narrative for clarity and comparative flexibility, functional utilities poignantly visualized by the diagram on Skocpol (appearing at the end of this chapter). Plotting sampled HS cases on x-y axes allows for simultaneous comparison within and between various theoretical and methodological denominations in a manner that captures interesting overlaps which would otherwise have remained hidden with Smith. For example, while theory may unite neo-Marxists Thompson and Anderson versus neo-Weberians Eisenstadt and Bendix at one level, method or use of comparative historical technology provide reason to realign Thompson and Bendix against Anderson and Eisenstadt. Finally, far more than Smith's, Skocpol's anthology, while perhaps being less extensive in coverage, lends access to intensive critical, rather than just descriptive, examination of the sampled works nonetheless.

At this point, the odds in our cost-benefit calculation appear to fall strongly in favor of Skocpol. On these grounds, a beginner, who can only afford one of the maps, may reasonably go for Skocpol, with this rookie's warm blessings, but not without first cautiously reading the critical fine-print or disclaimer before buying the merchandise. Not unlike Smith's, the particular underlying rhetorical premises of Skocpol's map lead if inadvertently to the downplaying of important nuances.

Just as Smith dramatizes his argument on politics/ideology in terms of coherent phases and big think issues at the expense of methodological nuances, Skocpol's attempt to put the normative argument across in favor of her vaunted third research strategy, and within it those subscribing to the Millian 'method of difference' (like Skocpol herself), makes her prone to deflate variations and inflate the semblance of coherence within designated strategies to more dramatically bring out differences between them. Vindictively, Smith's comparisons of Moore and Skocpol's (considered by the latter as choice-cut cases of analytic macro-causal HS strategy) reveals two major cracks on the parchment of her map and main argument.

Firstly, in emphasizing coherence by sorting for example hypothesis-testing HS cases under either one of two categories (MoA vs MoD), she may be labeling her own agenda correctly, yet falsely designating others like Moore, whose use of comparative method hardly complies with any of these terms. For as Smith notes, Moore employed cross-national comparisons primarily as a way of testing, and often rejecting, potential empirical generalizations which might explain specific cases. So, for instance, in his *Social Origins of Dictatorship and Democracy* (1969), Moore mobilizes two basic tactics: a) comparison of cases in which a hypothesized cause is present, but which differ in regard to the outcome one seeks to explain (Germany versus US); b) case comparisons in which the relevant outcome shared by various potential causal factors were found only in some and not all cases (France cum

Germany).

In this sense, Moore's practice deviates from Skocpol's Millian recipe, combining, as it were, the methods of agreement (MoA) and difference (MoD) engaged in e.g., *States and Social Revolutions* (1979), implying, on the one hand, juxtaposing by MoA three otherwise different cases (France, China and Russia), but having in common both the hypothesized causal variables and outcome to be explained, and contrasting by MoD, on the other, this first 'positive' set of cases to a 'negative' set of cases (Great Britain, Prussia and Japan) otherwise similar to the first set, but neither containing hypothesized causes nor produced the outcome to be explained (i.e., revolution).

Secondly, co-extending with the first, the advantages she attributes to MoD, may, upon closer scrutiny, turn out to be overrated, which, as Smith suggests, gives practically little allowance for 'encountering data that contradict the initial thesis' in as much as MoD departs by design from cases in which both hypothesized causal factors and the outcome to be explained are absent, as elaborated above. Together, noted cracks compromise in no insignificant way the stability of Skocpol's normative argument.

Ergo, a last word of advice to beginners. If you can only afford one of the two maps, Skocpol's would make an excellent choice, but do read the fine-print, and do borrow a copy of Smith from the library as reference and visual aid to magnify the hidden text.

Diagram 1.

Theory, Method and Research Strategies in Historical Sociology (HS),
Theoretical Orientation/Writer (*y*), Research Strategy (RS) 1-3 (*x*)

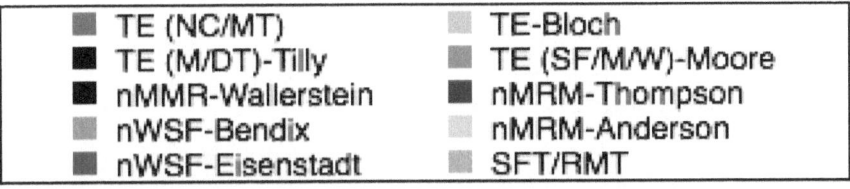

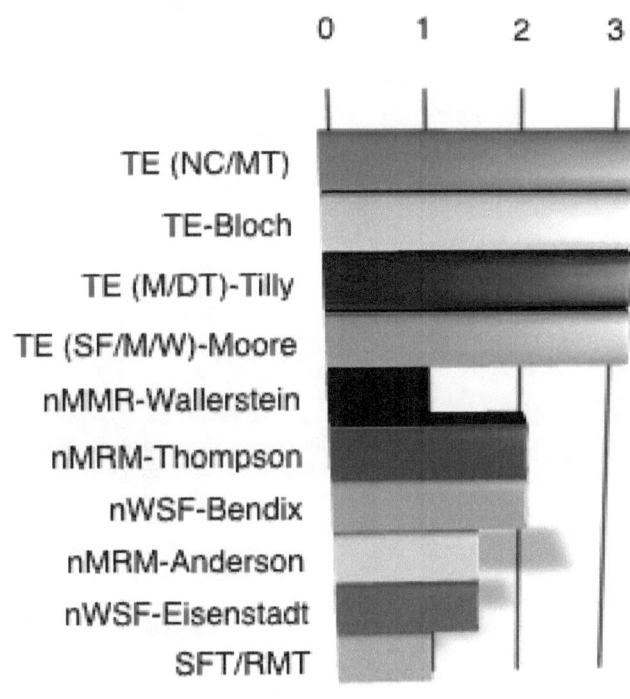

Notes on Diagram 1
Theory, Method and Research Strategies in Historical Sociology (HS)

y-axis denominations (theoretical orientation/writer)
SFT/RMT = Structural-Functionalism/Marxian Economism
nWSF = neo-Weberian Structural Functionalism
nMRM = neo-Marxist
TE (SF/M/W) = Theoretical Eclecticism (Structural Functionalism/Marxist/ Weberian)
TE (M/DT) = Theoretical Eclecticism (Marxist/Durkheimian)

x-axis denominations (research strategies)
1 = application of general models to history
2 = application of concepts strictly to interpret history
3 = analyzing causal regularities in history

Theoretical orientation:
From bottom-up on the y-axis, the various denominations indicate that all nine relate to theory of one form or another. In fact, most if not all of them developed historical critiques as a reaction to the a-historicism of the then dominant discourses of Parsonian functionalism and its extension in evolutionistic modernization theory, Marxian economism, and neoclassical economics. A rereading and conceptual reworking of classic think proceeded from this confrontation. Thus, we find critical advocates like Eisenstadt and Anderson reworking Weberian and Marxian concepts (i.e., historical bureaucratic empires and the absolutist state) to 'de-Parsonize' SFT & 'politicize' RMT, respectively; critical rejectionists like neo-Weberian Bendix & neo-Marxist Thompson bouncing historical cases off SF & Marxian class theory to show that they don't work. While none of these four churn out any new set of explanatory generalizations, Wallerstein & Tilly do, with the former replacing Marxist theory of capitalism with his world-systems model, & the latter testing Maxist & Durkheimian assumptions to explain the connection between classic issues of and long-term processes like Western commercialization, industrialization, state formation & collective action. Polanyi, Moore, Bloch are theoretical eclectics like Tilly, who try to make sense of historical patterns using whatever theoretical resources are suitable for this purpose.

Research Strategy & Method:
On the x-axis, selected writers are matched with one or some combinations of the three identified operational procedures by which to bring theory and history to bear upon each other. The logic of method adds further nuances to y-axis theoretical orientations. While comparative history (single or multiple case comparisons) of one sort or another is standard technology across these procedures, distinct applications add up to different mixtures between theory & history for each strategy. With Strategy 1 (RS1), where historical comparisons are used to demonstrate the rectitude of a given theory at one extreme, and Strategy 2 (RS2), where theoretical concepts and dramatic historical case contrasts are used mainly to clarify particularities or make meaningful historical interpretations, at the opposite end, we have Strategy 3 (RS3) at midstream, where historical comparisons are deployed to test or develop causal generalizations. (SMT? or SFT) as exemplified by Smelser makes for an open & shut case of RS1; Bendix & Thompson are transparent cases of RS2; Eisenstadt & Anderson operate on the margins by supplementing RS2 with a bit of RS1(using comparison to highlight particularity and theory to capture, but not fully pursue or test the logic of that particularity); Wallerstein's historically encompassing model incorporates a bit of RS2 but falls in the end within the radius of RS1; Polanyi, Bloch, Moore & Tilly all move towards RS3, yet applying different comparative historical tactics to generate or test causal explanations and hypotheses.

3

TIMING THINK
THINKING TIME

MAKING SOCIOLOGY TICK

CLASSIC & CURRENT CASES OF
BIG THINK, BIG TIME & COMPARATIVE TECHNOLOGY

Historical Sociology, as Abrams, Smith, Skocpol and Tilly in the previous chapter tell us, is all at once vision and practice. Yet, as we've learned from them too, the ideal marital union between sociological theory/concept and history, in both past and present tenses, has in practice been a poly rather than monogamous affair; multiple arrangements along a finely-graded scale of disparate Historical Sociology types. As earlier noted, scale variations derive basically from the way individual historical sociologists execute the standard operational procedures of big think, big time, and comparison (cf pp. 2-3)

With the road maps tucked safely in our travel-bag, we will next venture into the *terra firma* to pick up the scent of these three basic elements in the unique historical sociologies of Weber, Therborn, Tilly and Zelizer. Weber will be paired against Therborn here to contrast the prospects and problems of deductive and inductive approaches, and their ramifications on noted operational procedures. Tilly and Zelizer are set in the next chapter to meet in a friendly sparring match to mark the difference between the quintessence of big-think-big-time-big comparative practices as opposed to new, more prudent medium-scale agendas. Individual and collective match scores within and between these contesting pairs will be critically tallied in a concluding comparison.

MAKING EUROPEAN MODERNITY TICK
TOP-DOWN OR BOTTOM UP

WEBERIAN DEDUCTIVISM VERSUS
THERBORNIAN INDUCTIVISM

WEBERIAN TOP-DOWN HISTORICAL SOCIOLOGY

A preview of what probably constitutes one of the earliest and most explicit attempts to develop an HS research agenda can be extracted from Hans Zetterberg's anthology of Weber's (1986) central essays on the origins of Western capitalism. Logo-typical of this classic agenda is the reciprocal application of top-down precision-made sociological concepts or 'ideal-types' to explain particular historical patterns and multiple case comparisons to achieve maximum dramatic historical contrast. In Skocpol's chart, these reciprocal features would locate Weber somewhere in the vicinity between research strategies two and three. Quickly, let's track down the footprints left behind by Weberian methodology.

In his essays, the big think Gordian knot Weber seeks to untie is: what made European or Western 'civilization' the original home of modern (rational) capitalism? To solve this legendary riddle, Weber directs the cutting edge of detective work at the hitherto unanalyzed dimension of cultural value-systems and their strategic impact on capitalist economic development at large. Putting Marx on his head,[18] he argues that more than elsewhere what turned the wheels of modern capitalism logically more in favor of the West was the early and ubiquitous spread in all realms of society therein (both as a system of thought and organizing everyday human activity) of what Weber called an 'economic spirit' or 'ethos' (i.e., an instrumentally calculating long-term profitability think), which in turn was, to borrow a Marxian metaphor, conceived in the 'womb' of ascetic Protestantism's rational ethics.

Step by step, Weber makes this argument run using the clockwork concept of 'rationality' (-sation) and multiple cross-case comparisons, either horizontally between contrasting types of 'civilizations' or religious/ethical systems, or vertically between traditional and modern types of capitalism over time within Western 'rational civilization' at each turn.

Thus, he begins the investigation by defining and deriving at the outset the theoretical and operational meanings of rationality and rational capitalism. Initially, he concentrates on the former term to mark the distinction between two main types—value versus purposive or instrumental rationality.[19] Theoretically, Weber contends that while both types have operated in most cases, modern 'civilizations' set themselves apart from others by striving for maximum instrumental and minimum value-rationality. Illustrating the point empirically,

---

[18]In the sense of developing the argument from 'super-structural' (cultural/ value structures) down to 'structural' pre-conditions rather than the other way around, as Marx did.

[19]Denoted respectively by action governed by non-negotiable ideals and following a vocation or moral principle irrespective of results versus action dictated by practical results and conforming with a code of responsibility in the sense that actors are answerable to the consequences of their acts.

he draws a rapid ('timeless') comparison between Western and Eastern (China and India) 'civilizations' as articulated in terms of science, art and culture, religion and politics, to demonstrate the striking presence and absence of instrumentalism in the former and latter case(s), respectively. Next, he cuts the analysis vertically within Western 'civilization' to contrast (this time switching on the time dimension) the 'epoch' of modern 'rational' capitalism from its antecedent pre-seventeenth century equivalent according to a tight, formal set of criteria.[20]

Three institutional preconditions or causal factors drawn from this set immediately conspire to make noted 'epoch' work: 1) instrumental rationality in finance, technology, work organization and distribution; 2) a modern constitutional state;[21] 3) a universal 'economic ethic.'[22] It was the conjuncture of these factors that made modern capitalism with its rational industrial corporate organization a unique Western experience, and within it, a unique epochal experience!

Again, to illustrate the argument, he compares Western with

---

[20]For this 'epoch' to qualify as full-fledged modern 'rational' capitalist, six basic conditions should be satisfied: 1) the total institution of 'free property rights'; 2) the total mobility of production factors in a 'free market;' 3) the predominant availability and use of rationally calculable technology; 4) the availability and delivery of 'rational' service of justice; 5) the predominant availability of 'free labor;' 6) a fully commercialized market economy. Overall, during this epoch, the rule of exclusively directing satisfaction of basic needs via market opportunities and rentability shall have been fully consolidated.

[21]i.e., with citizenship-knowledge, impartial bureaucracy and contractual legislation with predictable judicial decisions.

[22]i.e., where one no longer distinguishes private transactions with strangers from those with friends, acquaintances, kin (the despicable economic 'double standards' of Weber's pre-rational pre-capitalist societies), and rests on the fundamental principle of systematic profitability.

Eastern (again, China and India) cases to show that while the latter did contain the seeds of 1 and 2, full-blown development towards capitalism was held back by dominant kinship and caste-based value systems, aborting the expansion of a single-standard capitalist economic 'ethic.' And to demonstrate epochal differences and argue against received tenets on the origins of Western capitalism (against Marx's stress on productive relations and Werner Sombart's war-made-capitalism thesis), Weber again returns to the comparative East-West cases to show that while both did make war, the growth of luxury consumption rather than war-driven demand gave primary impetus to capitalist enterprise, in general.

However, whereas ostentatious aristocratic consumption in the Eastern cases met through coercive non-economic means (forced taxes and corvée labor) failed to produce sustainable modern capitalist organizations, in the West where this was as a general rule first achieved, the relative success rates among cases (e.g., England versus France) depended on the extent to which the 'democratization' of luxury consumption occurred. Hence, the 'mass´-ification of demand if you like (and correspondingly the growth of modern capitalist production) evolved earlier and faster in England than in France precisely because it was there that Weber's ideal-typical 3-D rationalization first took place.

If conjunction accounts for the exclusivity of Western rational capitalism in spatial (cross-cultural) and temporal (cross-epochal) terms, what in turn made all the pieces of conjunction fall into place? This leads us to the fountainhead of Weber's argument, that all things being equal, ascetic Protestantism's rationalism presupposed the expansion and consolidation of a universal capitalist spirit or economic ethos and logically thereby the rise of Western capitalism at large.

Dress-rehearsing the argument, he then traces the evolution of Protestant voluntary practices since the fourteenth century

Anabaptist introduction of adult baptism to show how they were gradually able to combine belief in God and Mammon, as opposed to other contesting Western religious systems like Catholicism.[23]

Having established the differences within, Weber takes the argument finally out for his usual cross-cultural spin to compare five ideal-type world religions (Confucianism, Hinduism, Buddhism, Christianity, Islam), with the view of illuminating how apparently similar economic organizational forms could be linked to sundry types of economic ethics, which could, according to their distinctive characteristics, lead to diverging historical outcomes. He finds that among these cases, only within three of them—Indian karma-thought, Zoroastrian dualism, and Calvinist predestination doctrine—could rationality exist free from magic and charisma, at least among a small group of religious virtuosos.

However, unlike the Eastern virtuoso who took to orgiastic, meditative practices as a means of escaping the meaningless-ness of this-worldly activity, the Western puritan sects incorporated the latter, creating ferment in favor of the systematic rationalization of everyday life, including eco-nomic activity. As this necessary normative factor was, despite the presence of other favorable structural conditions (potential market economies and state bureaucracies), absent in the Indian and Chinese contexts, sustainable capitalist develop-ment on par with the West was consequently subverted.

Lastly, on his recurrent and reciprocal use of ideal-type concepts and comparison to re-interpret history, Weber

---

[23]The crucial difference lay in puritan asceticism's 'this-world-fication,' individual-ization (and thus rationalization) of the sanctions and acts of contrition; in the latter, ultimate salvation remained an 'other-worldly' matter, the dispensation of which was the exclusive prerogative of a clerical elite and governed by a given doctrine rather than the lay individual's actual practice.

describes his distinct HS method as something mid-way between a purely typological study of religions and conventional historical research. For purposes of analysis, his study (via s-c ideal-typing) is compelled to be 'ahistorical' such that each case of religious ethics under review would consistently be treated as more homogenous than they actually were in the development process. Thus, ideal-typing intentionally leaves out an array of contradictions within individual religions, offshoots, in order to draw significant features in greater logical coherence (relations between religious/ethical systems and capitalism). This simplification would still be historically correct, as Weber avers, since stress is placed on those features decisive in shaping discrepant historical outcomes for all cases examined.

THERBORNIAN
BOTTOM-UP SOCIOLOGICAL HISTORY

What happens to European modernity after Weber? Therborn's (1995) piece grafts the postscript onto Weber's normative chapters, but elects to draft the postwar episode of modernity rather within the bottom-up format of what he dubs a 'Sociological History' approach. Intriguing about his agenda is its declared intention of neither expounding theory, re-interpreting history, nor for that matter testing hypotheses; something which, if we take his word for it, puts him beyond the range of Skocpol's 3-type grid under perhaps a fourth category of limited descriptive-empirical strategies. Let's examine Therborn more closely to see how he manages to pull the 'trick' of conveying the history of modernity allegedly in terms 'not so much a story as a series of video installations or as a set of exhibition exhibits." (Therborn, p 2)

Reading Therborn's installation manual in the first part of the book on "Theory and History" (chaps 1-2), where he sets the terms of the 'exhibit,' we recognize a curious mix of familiar Weberian steps and bold new departures. For him, the overriding issues are: what does European society look like?; how has it changed in the recent half century, and why?

As noted, he organizes the 'exhibit' on these questions around the concept of modernity, yet unlike Weber, Therborn invests it with a distinctively temporal rather than institutional meaning[24] to better suit his primary empirical concerns. As such, modernity is defined in terms of a prevailing concept of time as an 'epoch turned to the future conceived as likely to be different than the present and the past.' After making the concept literally 'tick' this way, he then situates Europe—in a bid to atone for the normative biases of single-trajectory models à la Weber or modernization theory—in the general history of modernity as one of four ideal-type routes (which incidentally are also actually existing trajectories), according to how modern political rights evolved in each case. Without elevating the endogenously induced class-based European path to the rule, this typology allows for less value-laden comparison with other distinct, equally justifiable historical routes marking the New Worlds, Colonial Zone countries, and those like Japan with externally induced, but selective, self-imposed modernization.

The empirical alarm sounded off by the rhythmic ticks of Therborn's concept and typology begs in turn two major questions. What happened to European modernity and to modernity itself? Is it still there, or has it ended or been superseded by what is fashionably referred to in current discourse as 'post-modernity'?

---

[24]As the case has been with Weber, Parsonian structural functionalism and modernization theory. Rather than defining modernity in terms of certain concrete institutions and social conditions (cf Weber), a procedure vulnerable to the pitfalls of 'institutional fetishism, and making certain specific institutional forms the hallmarks of a universal epoch,' Therborn's proposed concept leaves the latter more flexibly as causes, effects or contingencies for investigation.

To be able to turn off the buzzer with measurable answers to these issues, Therborn is thereby compelled to first derive (via macro-sociological theory) and specify the object, range and scope of measurement in terms of what strategic variables or dimensions of society (and their proper indicators) signify modernity, the change of which he intends to measure over time. Whether forward-looking European modernity is dead or alive will depend on observable shifts along the variables and dimensions indicated in his left-to-right running schema below. (p. 34)

By breaking down the modernity concept into quantifiable units, Therborn, without explicitly admitting it, is in effect de-constructing Weber, re-projecting the crucial other components of his universal economic ethical system that by analytical necessity tend to be camouflaged, thereby making them measurable to boot.

In contrast to Weberian deductivism, Therbornian inductivism rather than asserting the legitimacy of modernity by sophisticated argument leaves conceptual sustainability almost entirely to the discretion of empirical evidence. He lets data relevant to his conceptual variables decide if indeed one could make empirical generalizations as to whether modernity is 'dead or alive.' It is probably dying or entering its post-modern state if data would indicate remarkable changes in the set of variables identified.[25]

---

[25]Hence, if and when structuration patterns marked e.g., by differentiated, specialized, (de-agrarianised?) tasks, relatively equal distribution of means, growth of rights and duties, are reversed in any protracted or substantial manner, it may then be justified to announce the advent of post-modernism. The same goes for European enculturation patterns: when the unique mixture between clear-cut individuality and solidarily constructed collectivity, of association, class and nation-state disintegrates, when cognitive frameworks warp (in terms of long-term stagnation of knowledge or denial of its cumulativeness), when instrumental values and norms are de-differentiated and subjected to increasing recourse to authority, then one may with probable cause infer the demise of the modern era.

Modernity to Post-Modernity? Therborn's Theoretical Framework

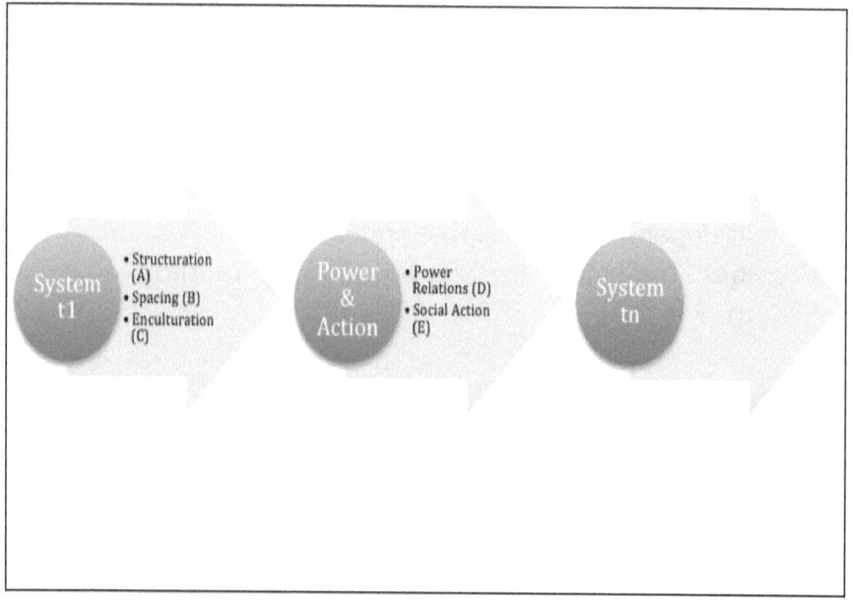

Notes:

A = formal & informal institutional resource endowment & constraints + chance set (risks & opportunities) over time as indicated by patterns of tasks, rights, and means.

B = territorial boundaries, distribution and configuration of resources & constraints (of A & C or economic & cultural space).

C = patterns of identities, cognitions (of knowledge & time), values & norms.

D = power distribution influenced by A-C, which in turn determines relative group capacities to social action.

E = actual translation of power relations into modes of individual & collective action, the result of which reproduces or changes the social system & completes the causal loop from one system to the other over time.

So in the succeeding 'exhibition screens,' and in conjunction with the letter and order of his theoretically derived schema (see *Appendix*), Therborn systematically proceeds in projecting comparative quantitative and qualitative data (if mostly from secondary sources and research surveys) on each of the noted strategic variables. Again, in contrast to Weber, Therborn's comparative technology departs more consistently from nation-state units (where Weber swings somewhat arbitrarily between 'civilizations' and nation-states), covers a wide range of cases (both intra-European and intercontinental, and within the former, Western and Eastern cases), and is mobilized not so much to dramatize contrasts for purposes of argument as to tease out in piece-meal fashion dialectical 'contradictions, dilemmas, tensions' along chosen variables for purposes of answering more open-ended empirical questions, intending as such to build a potential argument from the bottom-up. With inductive verve, Therborn submits theory to empirical interrogation as summed up by the forgoing chart (p. 34).

Tallying the trend-scores at the rightmost column of the chart in the concluding note, Therborn finds that European modernity (West + East) is as defined hardly 'dead,' but rather starting to descend from its highest state of growth (1940-1980s when the Cold War finally ended and post-industrialization began) towards a still unpredictable destination. A trajectory which may not necessarily be post-modern, but simply rather another type of modernity.

Perhaps one of the most central merits of Therborn's empirical collages rest on their prowess to expose modernity's historical paradoxes and contingencies. For example, the parallel development between East and West within Europe, the movement towards greater economic convergence in the West before but not after EC integration, the cultural resilience despite dramatic economic turns of traditionally strong collectivist public interventionist *cum* individualist family values.

As to why things happened as they did, it may, argues Therborn, be better explained by the historicity and contingencies of the European experience itself, rather than endogenous systemic dynamics as others, not least Weber, might contend. The way the War ended radically restructured means, rights and opportunities, reshaped continental political, economic and cultural space, and gave rise to new identities while discrediting others. This new account drew, however, from past features which made postwar continental modernity distinct from other routes: predominant industrial economies, internal conflicts and clear-cut class-based politics in tandem with weak kinship traditions more than elsewhere.

While indeed Therborn's indicators do suggest the blurring of classic class cleavages, the questioning of the future within Europe itself, and the rise of non-European conceptions of modern society in a manner that augurs that the dusk of modernity might well be setting in by *fin de siècle*, the final verdict, he believes, should best be left to future historians. The zeitgeist is, as he exclaims, usually 'schizophrenic'!

4

TIMING THINK
THINKING TIME

MAKING MODERNITY TICK LONG RHYTHMS & RUN LONG DISTANCES, MAKING MONEY RUN THE MEDIUM MILE

TILLY'S TITANIC COMPARATIVE HISTORICAL SOCIOLOGY

If you're looking for the epitome of long rhythm's prized hypothesis-testing macro-analytic Historical Sociology, there is undoubtedly no better candidate than Charles Tilly (although he himself would shun such epithet). His seminal *Coercion, Capital and European States* (1990) and *European Revolutions* (1993), along with other examples of Tilly's prolific scholarship, put sharp teeth to that reputation.

In other works, Tilly connects to those features and 'master' forces or processes so central to the making of modern European history—*industrial capitalism, urbanization, constitutional state bureaucracies, internal conflicts* and *revolutions*. True, some of these aspects or themes have surfaced in Weber and Therborn's works earlier on in this book. Yet, they were either treated ambiguously in Weber as ready-made items along with (and secondary to) Protestant-bred economic ethos on a check-list of requirements for full-fledged modern (rational) capitalism to operate, with neither so much as asking how they got there in the first place (e.g., constitutional states and industrial capitalist organizations), nor how these processes at a certain point in time apparently managed to push the whole lot of Europe along this single trajectory. Or, they simply had to be taken for granted, as in Therborn, since the focus and scope of the study brings him perhaps too far ahead of the fact (the question here is not what made for Western modernity, but rather whether it has indeed entered an entirely new era) to be able to do so otherwise.

Tilly tells the history of European modernity through the eyes of what he calls its 'epochal processes;' and he performs this task, as argued, not in a retrospective manner as the usual case has been, but in a 'prospective' one. He does this by taking a bold long-distance time-leap of a millennium (990-1992) and half of that (1492-1992) to chart, in the first instance, how multiple pre-modern state forms through exigencies of war finally converged along the modern trajectory of nation-states, and in the second instance, how these very same processes produced almost identical patterns in the career of European revolutions. In short, Tilly links in these works what long rhythm once attempted to explore in one, i.e., *States and Revolutions*; and by bringing these back to the forefront of analysis, he in effect critically emphasizes the theoretical primacy of politics and agency in the shaping of modern history.

Let's look then at how Tilly, with his reputed hypothesis-testing comparative method, argues the case on these purported links, coupled with the course he takes to test and prove that argument.

COERCION, CAPITAL AND EUROPEAN STATES

In this first case, Tilly poses the double-question: why a pronounced variety of state forms prevailed in Europe since 990 AD, and why these eventually converged towards different variants of the generic national state? Tilly confronts the problem with a set of twelve hypothetical statements, the essence of which may be reduced to a single stinging slogan: States Made War, and War Made States! However, while war in principle set the general direction and pace of state-making since 990 AD, in practice, the mode by which any state extracted from its territory and subject population the means of making it and the corresponding form of rule or state that took shape, varied at a given point in time and space. The defining parameters of noted diversity were accordingly the prevailing alignments of organized major social classes and their relations with the state, the balance of geo-political power relations within the international system of contending states, and, closing the loop, the level of technology and scale of war-making at large.

Three alternative modes or paths of resource extraction mark the long millennial career of European war and state-making. Along a modal continuum, capital (e.g., the Low Countries) and coercive-intensive (e.g., Brandenburg, Russia, Poland Hungary) modes occupy the opposite extremes with capital-ized-coercion (e.g., England and France) saddling the scale at mid-point. At whichever point on this typological scale a particular state ended up, ultimately rested on the intensity-ratio, i.e., the relative level and density of the two strategic variables of capital and coercion prevailing within territorial boundaries.

As a rule, in areas where city economies with their active capitalists predominated, capital-intensive modes of extraction became the most viable route. Conversely, where the landscape was carved by vast feudal estates with their powerful aristocracies, the odds tilted in favor of coercive-intensive modes. Later on, in a few areas where high concentrations of both variables evolved, a capitalized-coercion intermediate path opened up and eventually took the lead in war and state-making. The twin history of states and wars spanning the present millennium unfolded successively in four phases, each marked by unprecedented alterations in the capital-coercion equation.

Thus, between 990-1400 (the age of what Tilly labels patri-monialism) when relative capital-coercion concentration and accumulation levels[26] were still generally low and warfare was limited, low-scale and low-tech, coercive-intensive modes, with their comparative advantage at the given level of greater availability of coercive means—via tribute-taking forms of indirect rule—prevailed over an array of fragmented capital-intensive-run sovereign types (city states, city empires, urban federations, bishoprics; with greater availability of capital but nonetheless limited coercive capabilities operating mainly through urban militias).

Among tribute-taking states, monarchs extracted the capital they needed as tribute or rent, often within stringent contractual limits on the amounts they could demand from their subjects. They made war and mobilized the coercive means to do so mainly through armed retainers, vassals and militias who owed personal services to the crown, yet again with significant contractual limits. Gradually, between 1400-1700 (the age of s-c brokerage) as cities proliferated, rulers began in terms of capital to rely heavily on formally independent capitalists for loans, for management of revenue-generating enterprises, and tax collection. This sort of 'sub-contracting' resource mobilization and management arrange-

---

[26] i.e., there were still few cities and quite rudimentary, inchoate states to act as containers of capital and coercive means.

ment had its equivalent on the coercion side in the form of increasing use of mercenary forces supplied by contractors with relatively free disposition.

By the next phase, between 1700-1850 (the s-c era of nationalization), many sovereigns were incorporating the fiscal apparatus directly into the state and disenfranchising, in the opposite direction, independent contractors and their services, at the very point when mercenaries exited and huge locally recruited armies and navies entered the structure of national states. In the last phase (the s-c age of specialization) since the 1850s onwards, there occurred within states a sharper separation of fiscal from military organization and a hiking involvement in the management of fixed capital, again at the very point when citizen militaries backed up by large civilian bureaucracies were being consolidated (dovetailing well with the progressive splitting of police forces specialized in the use of coercion outside war). In the process, states changed from magnified war machines to multi-purpose organizations. Their efforts to control coercion and capital continued, but now in the company of a wide variety of regulatory, compensatory, distributive and protective activities.

As Tilly's account suggests, the general movement since 990 from indirect (tribute-taking and fragmented sovereignties) to direct forms (national states) of rule occurred on an exponential curve of rising accumulation and concentration levels in the capital-coercion equation, complying with the logic of war and the requirements of waging and winning it. When war-making dramatically scaled up from the second phase onwards, those who were earlier able to shift towards direct rule through national states, and among them, those who succeeded to gain the highest concentrations of capital and coercion also wielded competitive war-making edge over other national state rivals (or other state types for that matter) in an increasingly dense international state system. Leading national states' ability to effectively wage and win wars exercised a powerful push-pull effect upon others seeking to maintain relative positions of power within the European state system. Consequently, all roads eventually converged towards different variants of specialized, differentiated and multi-functional national states.

So how does Tilly engage this provocative war-state model? His first step is to establish by a sweeping comparative account (partially supported by quantitative data) of millennial changes in the ratio and relationship of European states and cities—the concrete representations or 'containers' of his two key variables, capital and coercion—that there is indeed enough implicating empirical evidence to build a case for the model at large and its component hypothetical statements. His findings appear to lend solid support to those premises: in as much as long-term data trends indicate that e.g., the hypothesized general upward movement and equalization of capital-coercion ratios did actually happen across Europe (as manifested by long-run city-state ratios),[27] these relationships

---

[27]Tilly's ratio count shows i.a. accelerating but fluctuating urban growth rate, which by the 1490s was paralleled by a relatively high but composite average population of states ranging from tribute-taking super-states to fragmented medium and micro-states or sovereignties (numbering roughly 200 states by any standard). While city-state ratio was at this juncture relatively still small (1:1-2), hence delimiting in general the level of accumulation/concentration for capital-coercion variables, the ratio altered dramatically by the 1700s onwards, which by the 1890s registered a total of around 30 states with an average of 60 cities per unit (by the latter half of the 1900s state population diminished to its present 25-28), all of which manifested different variants of national states. Re-interpreted by Tilly's model, relatively independent cities which at best propped up the coercive capabilities of states through 'sub-contracting' as it were, eventually got directly incorporated into the structures of a dwindling number, but territorially enlarging and directly ruling variants of national states. Those national states able to maximize the altering ratio most effectively via capitalized-coercion modes of extraction, also became the emulative models of state of the art war and state-making as well as industrial capitalist development.

did synchronize with parallel historical movements in the frequency (and the precipitous post-sixteenth century rise) of large-scale wars (shifting from sea to land-born warfare), often resulting in concessionary peace settlements and the significant redrawing of state territorial boundaries within an increasingly close-knit European inter-state system (reinforcing thus his geo-political hypothesis).

With the precision of his model validated, Tilly then more accurately exhausts the central war-made-state argument with a lengthy account of the mechanisms by which state rulers extracted the major means of war, and reciprocally, the implications of war for state structures. Here, he shows how states parsimoniously acquired exclusive control over the means of coercion from once powerful civilian armed forces. How escalating inter-state military conflict, particularly after the fifteenth century onwards, when war technology shifted from sea to land-born, from sub-contracted mercenary armies and navies to nationally integrated armed forces, raised the ante in favor of directly ruling national states and how states met the demands of war through different fiscal strategies (and how the choices they made were delimited by the extent to which their economies were monetized).

Next, Tilly highlights one of the most intriguing, unintended paradoxes generated by war in state-citizen relations, i.e. in the same way as the state's coercive and extractive capabilities by virtue of war and direct rule expanded tremendously, its legal obligations to subject-citizens and their enforceable rights and claims on the state inadvertently if remarkably widened (re-written in Tilly's dramatic prose as the militarization = civilization equation). Here, he traces the formation via state-citizen bargaining (and the differing conditions setting the terms and modes of bargaining which he illustrates with a few selected cases) of multi-functional national state variants.

Up to this point, a substantial part of Tillys' defense has been spent on proving that the general directions in the history of war-driven state formation drawn by the model along capital-coercion lines stand up to historical evidence. Hitherto, he has deployed comparative technology only extensively to dramatize those general points. In "Lineages of the National State' (Chapter 5), which I think constitutes the central empirical chapter of his work, he uses this technology more intensively by juxtaposing concrete cases of coercive (Russia, Poland, Hungary, Serbia, and Brandenburger states) capitalist (Genoa, Venice and the Low Countries) and capitalized coercion (the British Isles) trajectories. Through intensive comparison he tries to demonstrate that beyond the common preoccupation in war-making, diverging capital-coercion relations produced contrasting variants of the national state.

Penultimately, he moves on to examine how war not only made states, but also how it created an increasingly tight-knit European inter-state system, one whose operations constrain the action of its members. Lastly, Tilly reflects on contemporary relations between capital and coercion to understand why military men gained power in postwar states.

EUROPEAN REVOLUTIONS

Could it be that Tilly delegates too much responsibility to wars (and related external factors) for creating the history of states that he might just be miscarrying justice on other equally viable internal variables like revolutions? Couldn't one just as well invert the causality chain and argue perhaps to Marx's delight that class struggle and social revolutions were in fact the key creators of the history of class-serving states and, by the same token, of inter-imperialist state wars?

Not necessarily, as still Tilly seems to argue! Not if one edits the standard narrow connotations resonating from the concept and give revolutions, as he does in this work, a broader political (state-centered) definition as a forcible transfer of power over the state—with or without profound social transformation. With this adjustment, to which we will return below, Tilly is able to make his exploration and analysis of long-term historical patterns and variations in European revolutions in the past half-millennium (1490s-1990s) technically compatible with those he had previously un-covered in *Coercion, Capital and European States.*

In this sense, one may consider *European Revolutions* as the expanded annex to Tilly's chapter there on state-citizen relations, where he briefly previewed both questions and argument on routine political contention, state and revolution, and which he heretofore seeks to fully exhaust and develop. A task confronted through his typical hypothesis-testing comparative procedures.

As expected, Tilly starts by posing a set of strategic questions. To what extent and in what ways do great revolutions conform to the regularities of non-revolutionary politics (i.e., to routine political contention)? Particularly, how do broad changes in the organization of states impinge on revolutions between 1492-1992? Mainly, he argues that regularities in revolutionary history do derive from operational features of states independent of the former. Then, like clockwork, conceptual precision-making follows.

To the base-line definition above, a tight set of criteria is thus attached for sifting the wheat of true from the chaff of false or pseudo-revolutionary processes (RP): in the course of forcible transfers of power over a state, there should be *a*) at least two distinct contending blocs with incompatible claims to control the state; *b*) some significant segment of the subject population endorses the claims of each bloc (either single actors or coalitions). And to further make the concept time and variety sensitive Tilly adds that *c*) the new regime must hold power for at least a month and *d*) the smaller bloc must control at least one major subdivision of the state (geographic or admin-istrative). With such broader meaning, one could then empirically capture a wider range of events than our archetypal great revolutions, but still a much narrower range than civil violence, protest, rebellion or ephemeral transfers of power.

Moreover, as Tilly perceptively argues, insofar as revolu-tionary processes do not always hit home-runs from multiple sovereignties or open splits in polities to new state power, one has to distinguish between two key components: revolutionary situations (RS) and revolutionary outcomes (RO). Proximate causes for RS are the appearance of a) and b) above plus state incapacity or unwillingness to rule. ROs equate, of course, to effective state power grabs, which according to Tilly were most likely if there was substantial frequency of a) and b) plus if challengers manage to control extensive armed force. As proximate conditions may vary at any given point in time in the span of a RP, the RS and RO content in each case may vary and shift from one to the other.

Deploying these two main variables as tracers enables Tilly, not unlike his earlier attempts with capital-coercion ratios, to construct a typological diagram of revolutions, ranging from those with zero RS-RO (= routine politics) to complete (great revolutions) with intermediate variants and overlaps among them (top-down seizure, coups, civil war, revolts).

Historically, however, RS rather than RO has been the rule, and when power transfers do rarely occur, they tend to take different, usually contradictory directions, from socially radical to conservative modalities. Why the plurality but frequency of RS and the rarity but variety of RO? These empirical issues somersault to what actually made for the hypothesized RS-RO proximate causes, bringing us back to the first square questions and argument posed at the outset. Just as it did in the previous piece, this study approaches noted problems prospectively by looking at RP as a whole with the accent more on RS and less on the otherwise already well-emphasized RO.

By force of habit, Tilly, before empirically running the model against a number of selective comparative cases, first returns to the basic underlying argument, this time in full-length and with all the relevant ramifications. It is at this point we find the bridge that technically connects the two works, picking up and custom-building the current state-revolution argument from where it ended in state and citizenship in Tilly's previous piece.

Thus, Tilly contends that the past half-millennial history of state-making (and by extension, war-making) and capitalist development was decisive to European RPs insofar as it shaped the parameters in which strategic RS-RO variables occurred and developed. That is, the parameters of bargaining or claim-making between state and citizenry.

The development of capitalism and transformation of states intertwined to alter prevailing repertoires of claim-making, the nature of claims being made, the claimants and objects of claims. Generally, as earlier noted, as war-making high-scaled and rulers consequently went from indirect to direct resource management via national states, there occurred an ironic trade-off between higher state capital-coercion capabilities and greater civilian bargaining rights, concurrently moving from local to national claims on the state.

However, alternative paths, depending on actual capital-coercion intensity ratios in each case, produced different variants of national states and industrial capitalism, which in turn affected the timing, character, social base and outcomes of collective claim-making. Nevertheless, over the long haul of 1490-1990s, the general course and changing conditions of European claim-making synchronized with the growth of consolidated national states and capitalist expansion—as echoed by the nationalization of divisions involved in major conflicts, multiplication of claims bearing directly on state power, the proliferation of associational bases of collective action, and the increasing salience therein of class divisions inherent in industrial capitalism.

If one transposes this in the technical terms of Tilly's RP = RS + (RO) equation, one may be able to derive a continuum of RS-types on the basis of the distinct revolutionary coalitions they involved over time, as denoted by the kind of agenda (territorial versus interest) and the degree of direct relations (direct versus indirect) they fostered.

This typology runs the gamut from patron-client, military junta, communal anti-tax, dynastic, class-based, to national RS, the prevalence of which varied and overlapped over time and national context, yet followed in the end (consistent to the general direction of state formation) a similar trajectory towards more effective class-based and national RS-types.

It states the case poignantly: that massive changes of social organization as a function of state transformation between 1490s-1990s transmuted the conditions of the proximate causes undergirding RS and ROs. After installing the remaining fixtures to his framework, Tilly resorts to his comparative toolkit to empirically explore noted changes in a number of European RP cases.

The first set of cases illustrates the tenacity of Tilly's state-revolution thesis through an extensive (just as he did in the previous work) comparison of revolutionary track-records in a capital-intensive region (Low Countries, LC),[28] a coercive

---

[28]LC with strong city + weak nobility = RP spate between 1477-1877, with communal and dynastic RS and ROs particularly intense until 1600s, in 1830s ff two failed national RS, thereafter contained if tense liberal bourgeois politics.

intensive region (Balkans B and Hungary H),[29] and an intermediate one of capitalized coercion (Iberia I).[30] In each case, he finds the shift from often indistinctly merging communal, dynastic and patron-client to more clear-cut national and class-based RS, but along trajectories and schedules differing significantly as a function of discrepant capital-coercion (C-C) ratios. Observable in I and B, if not in LC, was also the extensive involvement of the military. The results appear to dovetail with Tilly's hypothesis: i.e., observed RP regularities and regional variations followed those of state formation and C-C ratios, respectively. RPs and non-RPs (routine political contention) varied concurrently from region to region and period to period. The three cases further reveal the affinity of war and revolution, where one not only stimulated but merged, if imperfectly, with the other.

After quality-checking his main hypothesis for potential fine-tuning in this manner, Tilly now applies it and related

---

[29]B and H = weak nobility and bourgeoisie coupled with shifting fragmentation of sovereignty; Ottoman imperial expansion and contraction set the rhythms of RPs, the prevalence of conquest and territorial expansion obscured the lines between war and revolution here more than elsewhere. As a rule, dynastic (1500s) and peasant communal RS (1500-early 1900s) often fused, but the latter appeared autonomously whenever imperial power faltered. National RS occurred early and frequently, while until recently class-based RS rarely arose without a strong element of nationalism (e.g., Croatian-Serbian war).

[30]I = accurately speaking, capital-coercion combinations varied intra-regionally with strong nobility in countryside, privileged municipalities and heavily capitalist coastal regions = long survival of dynastic rule + extraordinary succession of RS between 1700-1930s. Here the track from communal to national RS ran askew with the early start of national RS/RO, but based on privileges and treaties (1500-1600s) to dynastic + class-based + military junta types (1870-1900s). A difficulty encountered in Tilly's account in this particular case is that one loses sight of Iberia being of the capitalized coercion mode in some parts of the text. He subjects this case to identity crisis when he haphazardly refers to it as a case of coercion-intensive producing RP (e.g., in the chapter on the British Isles, Iberia is clearly labeled as such).

framework more intensively to the comparative cases of the British Isles (capitalized coercion state trajectory), France and (capitalized coercion or capital-coercion intensive; where labeling appears to be ambiguous here as well as in the case of) Russia (coercion-intensive). While using the same periodization, he magnifies the analysis one century in each area (1600-1700, 1750-1850 and 1850-1900), respectively. The bulk of his data is drawn from secondary literature, particularly from the chronologies of war and revolution by Jack Levy and van Luard plus supplements.

The British case of high intensity RPs (between 1492-1603) registered a mix of overlapping dynastic struggles, anti-tax communal rebellions and resistance to religious innovations (in England, Scotland and Ireland), which directly reflected the ways in which Tudor rulers were reshaping their state increasingly along capitalized coercion lines (eventually succeeding to combine a strong sovereign with considerable sway over the armed forces, a relatively autonomous parliament and a stable alliance between landlords and merchants). It also revealed varying RS conditions within British satellite-states (Ireland, Scotland, Wales) fueled at least until the 1740s by the English drive to incorporate them into her structure. Pending state consolidation, the struggle in the major catalogue of RS over the century reviewed thus often straddled the boundary between war and revolution. Yet, as the state managed to consolidate, it was concomitantly able to contain RS as the growing prominence of parliament re-channeled popular struggles from direct attack of the state to legislative reform at periods close.

Compared to the British, Iberian and Balkan cases, France experienced fewer RS; and this may, following Tilly's statist logic, be attributed to the early success of French rulers in welding a large space into a single centralized if bulky state more than in the former three cases. Like the British though, France had its taste of repeated dynastic, anti-tax communal and combinations of the two (plus religious) conflicts at least until the 1650s; ebbing during the 1700-1800s but with few spectacular class-based RS (a series of French revolutions since the first in 1789). In the long-run, France, like in Britain, became decreasingly prone to full RS just as national-level politics and the state became increasingly well-organized and consolidated. Remarkable for this case has, discounting Francophone colonies, been the scarcity of national RS since the 1490s, not least due to early Crown attempts at cultural homogenization of the citizenry, thereby liquidating national claimants to state power.

From France, Tilly shifts eastward to coercive intensive Russia, the paradigm of early super-state formation through aggressive wars of conquest, the latter of which overlapped with and fueled intermittent rebellions. Here, conquests and the need to sustain them lead sixteenth century czars to inadvertently construct a massive, expansible system of patrimonialism at the top, indirect rule in the middle, and a growing class of serfs under the control of state-backed landlords at the bottom.

Subsequent wars transformed that structure chiefly by thickening it, setting the pace and rhythm of open RS (dynastic, patron-client and communal peasant struggles) that on the average broke out once every decade between 1550 and the Napoleonic wars. As the state consolidated, however, RS declined only to be punctuated by the celebrated class-based revolutions of 1905 and 1917-1918. In this regard, the closest approximation of a national RS took shape only recently during Gorbachev's era and the debacle of the once formidable Soviet state organization.

In the concluding note, Tilly, besides claiming general valida-tion of his argument, also draws other interesting and unex-pected lessons from the comparative illustrations. One crucial discovery was that a few non-revolutionary episodes (i.e., no open polity split or RS) did sometimes yield ROs, for instance, during monarchial restoration by virtue of general war settlements, when powerful outsiders intervened in national politics, or when an existing state was conquered by another totally different state. In all cases, rapid top-down installation of new ruling coalitions occurred.

Revolutionary Situations (RS) types
according to period & coalition formats

RS type	Period	Coalition format
Patron-client based	1500-1600s	client communities & landlord patrons align against crown rule
Communal revolutions	1600-1800s	constituted community-based (peasant villages, craft guilds & religious orders) anti-tax coalitions, particularly during military build-ups
Dynastic	1500-1700s	intra-elite coalitions involving landlords with dynastic claims to rule /articulated in repeated succession struggles besieging European monarchies)
Class-based	1700s ff	conforms with Marxist model, albeit incorporating struggles where ruling class segments took part
National	1700s ff	like communal RS, relying on contiguous populations, but at a much larger scale with more complex division of labor among intellectuals, political entrepreneurs, military men & common members of a putative nationality
Military junta	1900s ff	Alliance with some dynastic faction or fragment of the bourgeoisie

Another more puzzling finding, recalling Tilly's RS continuum arraying connections with their social bases, was that, contrary to expectations, the specialization of state structure and growth of interest politics on a national scale did not reduce the importance of shared territory as a basis for revolutionary solidarity. Right up to 1992, putatively national groups rather than class coalitions or other aggregation of interests remained the most common launchers of deep challenges to existing European rulers. Tilly dignifies even this with a state-centered explanation: the same processes that made national statehood more valuable, pivoted it at one level on claims to common origin, and at another, excluded from national politics populations claiming common origins other than those authorized by the state.

ZELIZER'S DWARFIER HISTORICAL SOCIOLOGY

Zelizer's *The Social Meaning of Money* (1994), reminiscent of the previous pieces, tunes Historical Sociology in on the frequency of one of capitalist modernization's most celebrated but analytically clouded 'master processes' and tropes (representations)—monetization and money. Mainstream utilitarian approaches of different stripes, from Marx, Simmel, Weber to Bellah and Habermas, have all tended to desocialize the meaning of both processes and medium by viewing money as a single interchangeable, absolutely impersonal instrument—the very essence of Weber's rationalizing civilization—and overrating the consequences of its irresistible spread as something which inexorably homogenizes social ties.

Such economistic view reinforces and translates into the aphorism that everything money touches turns into the gold of calculating economic rationality. Zelizer seeks to dispel this commonly held myth by examining changes in the public and private uses of money in the US between 1870-1930, to argue and show indeed how at each step of money's advance people have infused social meaning into that process. Among others, people have reshaped their commercial transactions, introduced new distinctions, invented their own special forms of currency, earmarked money in ways that baffle market theorists, incorporated money into personalized webs of friendship, family relations, interactions with authorities, and forays through shops and businesses.

In effect, Zelizer reformulates the 'money-problem' into something like: just as money commercializes, and to that extent, de-socializes, the meaning of interpersonal relations so do people re-socialize the meaning of money at every turn.

Aside from the more obvious counterweight this manner of re-problematizing the meaning of money poses to Weber's concept of instrumental rationality, her Historical Sociology provides an interesting contrast to Tilly's agenda. Whereas both share the basic ingredients of big think's hypothesis-testing HS formats, Zelizer runs her argument and analysis at a somewhat lower altitude than Tilly's. Unlike his inclinations to 'master processes,' massive multiple case comparisons across time and space, she focuses not so much on master processes as on their sub-processes (viz., the impact of monetization on selected spheres or networks of social relations and vice versa), single case yet multiple sub-unit comparisons (three types of social spheres or networks in the single case of the US) within a more medium-term time frame (sixty year span). Let's now go straight to how she navigates the main thesis along these lines.

As noted, Zelizer sets out to discredit the widely held utilitarian reductionist model of market money to which she counterpoises a five-point alternative 'differentiated model of money.' This model assumes: a) the co-existence of market and extra-market money, both profoundly influenced by cultural and social structures; b) the non-existence of any single uniform generalized money, but rather the existence of multiple monies, whereby people earmark different currencies for many and all types of interactions; c) that certain monies can be indivisible, 'non-fungible,' non-portable, deeply subjective and thus qualitatively heterogeneous; d) that the strict dichotomy between utilitarian money and non-pecuniary values is false; e) that the alleged freedom and unchecked power of money are improbable insofar as cultural and social structures set limits to the monetization process through profound controls and restrictions on the flow and liquidity of monies.

Zelizer then incorporates above premises into a reshaped concept of 'social monies' defined as objects having no common physical characteristics that by virtue of the uses and meanings people assign to them have recognized, regularized exchange value in one setting or another. In other words, she argues that to a significant extent, monies are indeed socially constructed. People adopt elaborate controls over money and establish differential earmarks when and where they are engaged in delicate or difficult social interactions and ex-changes. Such a case is nowhere more ironically stated than in the US, the emerging bastion of capitalism, where forms of money earmarking multiplied just as legal tender or official money became more uniform and generalized. Exactly with the US as case in point, Zelizer hopes to build a convincing case for the argument and show how, how much, and why the social earmarking of modern money was able to operate even where one might have least expected it to do so.

For strategic purposes, she time-frames the study between 1870-1930, a period marked by post-Civil War expansion of the economy, the rise of real per capita income and modern consumerism; one which created the means and incentives for differentiating monies. She culls her data primarily from contemporary qualitative sources, inter alia, minutes of court hearings, etiquette books, instructions for charity workers, annual reports of charitable institutions, a few relevant household budget surveys, consumer and home economics textbooks, women's magazines, etc.

Zelizer test-runs her model by exploring how increasingly monetizing US society affected three traditionally person-alized networks of social relations (the institutions of family, gift-giving and charity) and how they reciprocally deflected and recycled the intrusion of cash through the creation of changing and contested modalities of monies (domestic, gift and charitable monies). In the first instance (family), she examines the tensions involved in the definition, allocation and use of domestic currencies, focusing on the most debated household currency—housewife's income—and tracing its transformation as women became the family's consumer expert.

On the second count (gift-giving), she recounts how money, in the face of the early twentieth century modern consumerist onslaught, entered the highly personalized circuit of gift-giving, tremendously multiplying the magnitude, range and meanings of modern gift transfers and gift currencies. As gift exchanges expanded, gift money became no longer just family currency; within the household its differentiation from other domestic transfers occurred.

Outside the home, gift transfers, which used to be reserved for kin, friends and intimate relationships—where both donor and recipient exercised discretion by personalizing gift goods to certify the equality of exchange and the intimacy of the gift—also began to enter other more impersonal social circuits. Here, the intrusion of gift money led to complicated twists precisely because the call for display of intimate, affectionate knowledge of recipient and relationship contradicted to some extent the impersonality of the many other settings and relations in which money transfers took place. Under these conditions, gift money easily slips into veiled charity, payments or entitlements. To illustrate the workings of these principles and increasingly delicate social relations, Zelizer draws a comparative account of the contentious careers of Christmas bonuses, tipping and courtship gifts.

Next, she explores the official creation of charitable money and extends the analysis of the previous illustrations by showing the interaction of state, domestic economies and gift transfers. Here, Zelizer raises the problem of what happens when government deliberately sets out to break the homogeneity of money by visibly demarcating among kinds of monies as seen in the persistent conflict between cash and in-kind relief in social welfare policy. This conflict makes the argument even more graphic as it unfolded at the height of state attempts to standardize and homogenize legal currency right at the moment when the zeitgeist of modern mass consumerism could have easily legitimized cash-relief.

Deployed comparative cases appear to confirm the anxieties of Zelizer's hypothesis: that the social construction or earmarking of monies evolved even in the theoretically most vulnerable areas of social life, those susceptible to rationalization: domestic transactions, gift bestowals, and charity. As money penetrated these social networks, individuals and organizations 'invented' a spectrum of currencies—housekeeping allowances, pin money, spending money, money gifts, gift certificates, remittances, tips, Penny Provident savings, mothers' pensions and food stamps. Thus, while the market money model may perhaps correctly apply to certain market exchanges with developed sets of routinized transactions, they hardly capture how money operates in areas of more complex, less routinized social interaction. By focusing on small-scale counterparts of large-scale processes, Zelizer believes she has demonstrated how differentiation, innovation and contest are dialectically integral to the narrative of monetization.

5

TIMING THINK
THINKING TIME

CRITICAL THINK ON THE TIMING AND THINKING OF
HISTORICAL SOCIOLOGY

Finally, after our perspiring, harrowing run-through of four contrasting and remarkable examples of Historical Sociology craftsmanship, this rookie, partly dazzled by the shine of the handicraft, but no less suspicious of potential quality defects, will now try to put them on balance and play the role of trouble-shooting amateur clockmaker. We'll start with the shine (prospects) and end with the defects (problems and limits). Having done this amateur critical check-up, we will later consult the experts in the concluding section to get a more qualified opinion on standard HS design flaws and damage-control.

PROSPECT SCOREBOARD

Our gang of four serves us Abrams vision in fruitfully different flavors, prepared and cooked according to any one or a combination of research strategies included in Skocpol's map of the trade. Collectively, as this book's title (Timing Think, Thinking Time) playfully suggests, although they all 'make Sociology tick, and History think,' the way their individual craftsmanship actually combine 'tick' and 'think', History and Sociological theory, and the prospects that go with that particular combination, vary distinctively.

At a general level, the collective works reviewed here deliver high ratings in the innovative ways they are able to re-problematize the question of modernity and modernization. Beyond the standard HS drill applying sociological concepts to history and vice versa, as well as employing comparative technology to that effect, each work draws its comparative novelty and advantage significantly from the particular conceptual machinery or clockwork and analytical framework it uses and the effective range in which the latter is designed to run in time and space via comparison.

So tallying individual high-points on the prospective score-board, we get the following comparative results.

With his conceptual clockwork of instrumental rationality, Weber is able to liberate hitherto analytic mindsets from, as it were, the dictatorship of economic reductionism to highlight the relatively autonomous role of cultural, religious, value/ethical systems and processes as strategic variables in the making of Western modern civilization. At the same time, he lends us an innovative perspective that emphasizes context and conjuncture of multiple variables over single causal explanations, one that makes for dynamic comparisons across cases with apparently critical similarities, but where differences in actual strategic factor-mix lead to an acute variety of historical directions and outcomes (Western versus Chinese and Indian civilizations). However, as noted earlier, Weber's rationality concept tends to be a bit overstretched, theoretically and normatively overloaded in a manner that makes his clockwork inadvertently throb fainter 'ticks.' His analytical instrument makes the potential user vulnerable to the double standard of, on the one hand, historicizing differences between cases and, a-historicizing differences within those very cases, on the other.

A liberating contraceptive to this Weberian bias can be found in Therborn's 'de-institutionalized,' 'de-norm-ized' and more empirically sensitized concept of modernity. He repairs the clockwork as such to make it 'tick' louder by defining modernity in terms of a prevailing forward-looking concept of time. In contrast to Weber's a priori consignment of it to a presumed set of standard instrumentally rational, not only unique but comparatively more advanced structures, institutions and norms, Therborn measures and derives from this temporal definition, empirical changes and continuities in the structural institutional and cultural expressions of European modernity over the past half century. Instead of dead-end juxtapositions between an alleged single and successful format of or route to modernization (Western Europe) and a host of 'deviating' and failed equivalents elsewhere (e.g., China and India), his time rather than institutionally-oriented clockwork permits more open-ended comparisons between equidistantly operating, distinctively different formats of or routes to modernity: New World, Colonial Zone, Japan-like externally induced but selective, self-imposed versions.

Particularly, in the current era of global modernization, Therborn's multiple format perspective enables one to more clearly see possible points of interfacing, cross-fertilization or transmutations between laterally evolving systems of modernization (e.g., US, European and Japanese formats). With his clockwork, one is better able to capture historicized differences (and similarities, in a way that patches up Weberian deficiencies) between cases, and most importantly, historicized dissimilarities and similarities *within* cases (e.g., changing time perceptions with their sundry institutional articulations within Western Europe and between the latter and Eastern Europe).

Inevitably, of course, the comparative advantages of Weberian and Therbornian approaches to the problem of modernity or modernization should be weighed against the central objectives defining their respective agendas. For Weber, the main course on the research menu is to find an alternative general explanation to the origins and mechanics of modern Western capitalism. His way of angling the problem in 'super-structural' (culture, value-ethical dimensions) directions is one of Weber's most durable contributions and a vital counter-weight to economic reductionist models. For Therborn, the issue of why modern capitalism first rooted in the West has already become moot to more contemporary post-modernist claims of its irreversible senescence and actual demise. His contribution lies in the way he breaks this question down to measurable units to determine the rectitude of those allegations.

Tilly's war-state-revolution clockwork re-projects, combines and develops some of the central themes and innovative elements found in Weber and Therborn. So for instance, Weber like Tilly highlights the emergence of a rational constitutional state as a strategic unique feature of European modern civilization. Yet, unlike Tilly, he treats it statically in relation to his more dynamic ethical factor, and retro-spectively as something which sometime during mid-millennium sort of gelled everywhere on the continent into a single universal form. His search for an airtight ethical explanation to the origins of modern capitalism at large and the normative connotations inserted into the concept of state unfortunately cast a dark cloud of a-historicism on the origins and evolution of the modern state in its current predominant national form (*gestalt*).

Serving as an antidote, Tilly historicizes the state problem by 'de-norm-izing' and defining the concept more empirically (partially reminiscent of Therborn). As defined by him, a *state* is generally a coercion-wielding organization distinct from the household and kinship groups, exercising in some respects clear priority over all other organizations within substantial territories. As such, this term is able to embrace a variety of non-national state forms like city-states, empires, theocracies, yet excluding other governmental modes like tribes, lineages, firms and churches.

In contradistinction, national states are those which govern multiple contiguous regions and their cities by means of centralized, differentiated, and autonomous structures (one which equates more or less with Weber's constitutional state), thereby enabling one to distinguish national-states from a variety of other historical forms. Tilly's overhauled clockwork, cuts slack for a long-run 'prospective' trace on the process by which pre-existing multiple state trajectories (again partially reminiscent of Therborn) and lineages eventually converged on different variants of the modern national state. Even at this terminal point, Tilly avoids conceding variety to Weber's universal constitutional state format.

Tilly repeats this historicizing procedure in the conceptualization of revolutions. First, he crafts an empirical definition of revolutionary processes as political transfers of state power with a clear, delimited set of criteria to distinguish otherwise analytically often conflated revolutionary situations from revolutionary outcomes (thereby posing a refreshing alternative to narrow Marxist predisposition solo towards socially transformative revolutions).

Second, with the aid of this clockwork, he canvasses both the historical variety of revolutionary processes and long-run changes and regularities in their nature and character to show how different but commonly violent state-power shifts were eventually (albeit occurring at different points in time and space) supplanted by more orderly and peaceful transfers as a function of heightened state-citizen bargaining.

What might perhaps register as the central innovation in Tilly's collective clockwork on states and revolutions at the patent office is the way it technically brings out the rarely adequately analyzed links between acknowledged 'master' or 'epochal' processes of European modernity/modernization: urbaniza-tion, resource extractive modes and processes (economic and non-economic, cf Tilly's capital-coercion model), class forma-tion, state-polity, collective action, war-making, and inter-national geo-political transformations. Although without making any pretext to general theory-building, Tilly's long-run comparative historical examination of these interlacing processes 'piece-meal-engineers' in practice a potentially de-velopable war-based state-building model.

Another innovative but less 'linear' way of re-imaging the often dualistic movement of modernizing processes is embodied in Zelizer's clockwork of 'social money.' Despite their contrasting approaches to modernization, both Weber's and Tilly's agendas cater largely to huge mainstream structures and processes and tend to depict their development more or less along linear evolutionary lines—perceived either thru Weberian lenses as the single-trajectory movement from pre-dominantly traditional value to instrumentally rational modern civilizations, or even in Tilly's more nuanced optics as the multiple trajectory movement of traditionally fragmented and less functionally differentiated states to their modern national, consolidated and more functionally differentiated form, albeit with several variants.

Zelizer's smaller-scale approach to one of modernization's mainstream processes, monetization, offers a sobering pill to noted linear evolutionism and to big-process syndrome. By de-economizing and socializing the meaning of money, she succeeds to bring us not so much to the mainstream of this process (dominant formal, impersonal market transacting networks and institutions as the usual case has been with utilitarian approaches) as to its margins (i.e., informal, more personalized networks of exchange) and sub-processes. By highlighting these fringes, she is thus able to magnify the often hidden dual historical movements and acute contradictions involved in mainstream modernizing processes like monetize-tion, which, in one direction, increasingly corrupts personal networks of social transaction, the effects of which are recycled in the opposite direction into new forms of personalized social exchange.

With the above prospect scores in mind, how might a summary sales-talk to an imaginary student customer in search for an appropriate HS strategy to the general problem of modernization sound like? Of course, *pace* the customer's particular preference, this amateur shopkeeper and clock-maker would issue the following recommendations: If she wishes to further explore the role of cultural, religious, value/ethical factors in modernizing processes, Weber's clockwork and agenda serves as a useful critical starting venue. If her preferences resides in the political aspects of modernization, then Therborn's state-centered clockwork provides an insightful entry point for critical analytical global comparisons. If she wants to procure practical methodological tips on how to make cultural, economic, political and other expressions of contemporary modernity quantifiable and globally comparable, she will surely profit from Therborn's time-oriented clockwork and inductive approach.

If she seeks to deconstruct modernization's mainstream processes further down to its component sub-processes to get at dualisms and contradictions—e.g., how a non-Western modern society like Japan has apparently been able to synergize Weber's vaunted rational economic with traditional value-oriented ethos and cultural norms, or at a lower level, how time-honored patrimonial highly personalized norms and relations in fact conduce rather than constrain the economic efficiency and international competitiveness of modern Japanese corporations—which otherwise often remain submerged in predominantly linear accounts of development, then Zelizer's small-scale approach certainly offers tremendously helpful pointers.

PROBLEM SCOREBOARD

To anticipate any accusation of chicanery, it is however wise to cut the sales-talk at this point and draw the customer's attention to a number of defects this amateur clockmaker has jotted down on the problem score-board. These critical flaws concern two major areas, in fact, the two cornerstones of Historical Sociology agendas at large: the application of concepts (the proverbial clockwork itself) to history and the use of comparative technology to carry the argument. The former concern begs the question of the 'stretch-ability' and 'shrink-ability' or de-limitability over time and space of the central concepts employed. The latter will tackle the issue of the extent in which comparative evidence corroborate the arguments and claims of respective contributions.

CONCEPTUAL INSTRUMENTATION
'STRETCH-ABILITY' AND 'SHRINK-ABILITY'

Concepts are useful, indeed quite indispensable instruments in problem analysis. Tailored to illuminate a particular analytic problem, the application of concepts, from Weber's rationality/rational capitalism, Therborn's modernity, Tilly's state and revolution, to Zelizer's social money, usually involves licensed reduction and magnification of certain aspects, dimensions, processes and relations of complex wholes in the real world (cf 'idealtyping' in Weberian jargon). Yet, in exercising that license, historical sociologists expose themselves more or less to the common problems that go with privilege: that of conceptual 'stretch-ability' and 'shrink-ability' or de-limitability in time and space. Comparing the four, the acuteness of reciprocal stretch and shrink problems appears to correlate well with scale or the relative size of temporal and spatial units in which conceptual instrumenttation is designed to run and operate. That is, the degree of acuteness goes from high to low as one moves from Weber, Tilly, Therborn to Zelizer.

Stretch and shrink problems are relatively most crucial in Weber's agenda, where the concept of rationality and the ideal-types derived from it are programmed to run through whole 'civilizations,' as a unit which he only very vaguely defines as a distinct configuration of belief systems and modes of organizing human activity. He first stretches the rationality concept to cover the maximum of 'civilizations,' then shrinks them to a minimum of two distinctively contrasting types viz., predominantly value-based traditional versus largely instrumentally rational 'civilizations.'

Weber's stretch-shrink acrobatics provoke a host of knee-jerking questions, some of which our customer may already be familiar with. First, one may hazard the issue of whether rationality as defined in either one or both of its forms should be the only motivational basis of human action. What about action motivated by psychologically-rooted fear, hate, or those based on instinct and chance? Or, as Zelizer has taught us, actions contingent on intimacy as articulated within the household, in gift-giving, etc.?

Second, even if one conceded to Weber's rationality concept, how are we to concretely separate, determine, let alone measure the alleged predominance of one over the other of his two ideal-typical, yet in reality often indivisible rationalities in traditional and modern 'civilizations'? Indeed, this is not an insignificant point insofar as even Weber acknowledges the relative presence of both in all 'civilizations,' i.e., whether traditional or modern, certain actions do derive from non-negotiable norms, others from negotiable rules based on practical results. However, only in modern 'civilizations,' can one, as argued, supposedly find instrumentalism at its highest rate and most comprehensive level. Thus, other than a mechanical check-list of maximum standard features for 'rational capitalism,' Weber lends no clear clues to that effect.

The trouble with this check-list is as it invokes instrumental features which are essentially (and intuitively recognizably) Eurocentric, its application to other 'civilizations' will all too easily show their non-conformity with the list's deliberately, by license of ideal-typing procedures, maximum standards. At the same time, when you take Weber's maximum rule seriously (as far as the check-list tends to assume the consummation of instrumental rationalization at all levels of society) and apply it to component societies within his modern Western 'civilization,' not any single one of them would be able to satisfy its stiff requirements.

Third, and perhaps the most crucial caveat as sporadically noted before, is the timeless and spaceless character of Weber's clockwork. By fusing the concept of rationality with 'civilization,' he automatically erases potential variations in rationality ratios *within* units, thereby amplifying variations *between* units. The unscrupulous workings of his clockwork all too often tend to jeopardize the tenure of Weber's license for exercising the craft of ideal-typing.

A fecund way of bringing back time and space into the analytical forefront, can, as has been repeatedly noted, be found in Therborn's concept of modernity, defined as an 'epoch turned to the future conceived as likely to be different and possibly better than the present and the past.' In this sense therefore, Therborn rescues us from the troubles of Weber's traditional-modern dichotomy. There is now no doubt that modernity has, as future-oriented mind-sets, gone global, and that there are only variants of the same theme.

With this concept, we are able to forgo Weber's Euro-centrism and a-historicism and to compare different modernity formats definitely on more equal terms (including the formerly perceived backwaters of modernity, the s-c Third World). Although probably lesser than Weber, there are certain stretch-shrink problems here, nonetheless.

The first question Therborn's definition raises in our mind is how actually future-oriented (and comparable) are these varying modernity mindsets, and how and where are these generally modern but contrasting mindsets manifested? The issue of future-oriented time-perspectives might be more conveniently settled in the case of Europe or his New World variant, and Therborn does provide us with empirical indicators of modernity articulating, viz., in the processes of structuration (e.g., tasks, rights and means patterns), socio-economic and cultural spacing, enculturation, and collective action and social steering repertoires. Nevertheless, the issue becomes more complicated and problematic once we go down to his Colonial Zone or Third World turfs.

In this regard, there are copious examples to illustrate the analytic dilemma generated by Therborn's concept. To wit, if future-orientedness and hence modernity is translated at the level of economy in terms of growth in, for instance, sundry Middle-East societies, the meaning of Therborn gets at the same time seriously compromised at other strategic levels (past-oriented theocratic state structures and Quran-based legal systems in operation in this context).

Further, what formally on paper and statistical charts serves as would-be indicators of forward-looking modern perspectives, are, in many cases, operationally mitigated by powerful past-looking informal processes.

To illustrate this point. While the incumbent Philippine president's recently launched ambitious program to turn the country into a newly industrialized economy by century shift may well epitomize future-oriented think, the equation changes dramatically at the provincial level where the same program of industrial modernization is currently being carried out. Here, modernity is invariably recycled by backward-looking patrimonial oligarchies in a way that severely counter-vails the development of Therbornian forward-seeking modern means, rights and tasks. In one of these provinces (Cavite),[31] the incumbent governor has check-mated the purported effects of modern industrialization by e.g., establishing monopoly control through his own employment agencies over labor supply for foreign corporations in the newly installed export processing zones. In the process, he has been able to beef up his traditional position as oligarch and patron in relation to both modernizing capital and labor. Examples like this beg the question: what and whose future-oriented agendas does Therborn's concept refer to?

Moreover, in this sense, one can recognize, although in lesser doses than Weber, the linear development-think built into Therbornian modernity concept. By stretching modernity globally to emphasize contra Weber the plurality of forms, the concept more or less ironically reduces all of them to the rule of future-looking time-perspectives in a way that does not do justice to the duality of perspectives in some, if not, most cases.

Again the syndrome of linear development-think may be discerned in Tilly as well, but with its own peculiar stretch-shrink twists. They arise here, just as in the previous cases, in the application of central concepts—i.e., war, state and revolution. All three are basically defined in geo-political

---

[31]See Coronel, S (1995).

terms and are thereby technically interconnected by Tilly. Hence, states are coercion wielding organizations with effective control over a substantial territory and population; revolutions are open splits in polities which may or may not lead to state-power transfers (revolutionary situations/ outcomes); wars are armed interstate struggles over territorial control.

Analytically, all three are seen to operate as 'epochal processes' and are made to run the large time-lap of a whole millennium (war and state) and then a half-millennium (revolutions and states) and through the whole European continent. The object of this 'prospective' long-stretching exercise is to simultaneously capture historical variety and regularity in the development of these processes.

The first sign of stretch-shrink troubles crops up when these concepts are applied at the outset of this vast time-frame, i.e., when states were still inchoate with territorial and population coverage still relatively small and insubstantial even as territorial boundaries intermittently shifted. At this early juncture, the difficulties of distinguishing state from non-state situations redound even more sharply on the 'state-mediated' concepts of war and revolution.

As we shall later see, this problem has critical implications on Tilly's main argument and defense. Returning to the latter concepts, at the time when states were largely still incoherent and multiple sovereignties were the rule, the boundaries between war and revolutions (e.g. civil wars) were by the same token frequently indistinguishable. Tilly himself noted this in the case of the British Isles before the consolidation of English monarchial power over Scotland, Wales and Ireland. In such case, does one consider armed encounters between English suzerains and ruler/subjects of the other three as interstate or civil wars? Noted ambiguity is far from just semantics since Tilly argues in the first instance that war, not revolution, technically made states.

The second sign of trouble appears in Tilly's bid to capture historical variations in state trajectories through the auxiliary concepts of capital and coercion—variables defined and juxtaposed by him in a manner reminiscent of Fernand Braudel's distinction between city and state-dominated economies, or the Marxist division between economic and extra-economic forms of exploitation—which in essence distinguishes between city-based (capital-intensive), politically decentralized and rural or agrarian-based (coercion-intensive), politically centralized modes of resource extraction and roads to state-making. Once again, when these distinctions are applied to the first half millennium, a period of fragmented state geographies, demarcation problems erupt, specially in areas like the Iberian Peninsula where one may find relatively equal proportions of capital-intensive and coercion-intensive extractive modes.

This difficulty is symptomatized among others by short lapses of amnesia in Tilly's comparative discussion of revolutions in the British and Iberian cases, where he tends to refer inter- changeably to the Iberian case as an example of either coercion-intensive or middle-road capitalized-coercion state trajectories (see short note, f n 35 in original text).

Stretch and shrink quirks are of course the occupational hazards of more or less broad-stroking clockworks such as Weber's, Therborn's and Tilly's. But what about smaller scale merchandise such as Zelizer's social money? Damage-control by this amateur clockmaker strikes a general note of approba- tion. The way she stretches against unwarranted utilitarian shrinking of monetary forms to a single universal unit, the concept of money to include not only market but other kinds of currencies, formal or informal, limiting its application to a strict set of cases (social networks in a single country within a sixty year time-frame), shields her from the common dangers faced by the previous trio.

However, while she might escape those hazards, Zelizer tends to be more constrained from drawing general statements in relation to the utilitarian money theories she criticizes, precisely because of her project's limited scope; an advantage the preceding figures, specially Weber and Tilly, derive from their larger agendas and were willing to pay for. Problems with Zelizer have instead more to do with claim-proof procedures, to which we turn in the next section.

WALKING THE TALK OF CLOCKWORK: CLAIM-PROOF & COMPARATIVE PROCEDURES

While there are always dangers involved in the application of concepts, the gravity or levity of those dangers should be assessed within the context of actual claim-proof and comparative procedures enlisted in each case. This tells us whether and how much each clockwork 'walks the talk.'

Let's start the trouble-shooting drill in the same order once again. Weber's agenda makes two basic arguments. The first, a differentiating one, the second a central one, a contextualized causal argument. That is, he argues that modern Western 'civilization' differs from others in terms of the omnipresence of instrumental rationality at all levels of society. Modern 'civilization' in its highest form, rational capitalism, ultimately took shape in the West at a point when instrumental rationalization along economic, political and ethical dimensions converged.

Although all three were equally important, the wide spread of an economic spirit or rational ethical system constitutes as argued the dynamic force behind the birth of capitalism. This ethos was the main missing link in the development of comparative 'civilizations,' which could otherwise have become capitalist. In the West, such economic ethic germinated within and developed earliest in the areas where Protestantism became the ruling religion.

The first argument is simply illustrated through a very fleeting comparison of Western and Eastern civilizations (in terms of art, music, science, etc.) and in a manner that forces and anticipates the issue and conclusion of rationality differences. Remarks like Western music is instrumentally rational because of its more complex and calculable features, whereas Eastern equivalents comparatively manifest their basic value-rational orientation as a function of their much simpler structure and form, is, to say the least, simply inadmissible as evidence.

Weber defends the argument on conjuncture again by contrasting Western and Eastern cases, first, to illustrate significant similarities and differences in economic, political, and most importantly, ethical systems; second, to demonstrate the inherently this-worldly inner-qualities, and thus, instrumentally hospitable character of Protestantism over the generally other-worldly qualities of other and even comparable religious systems. Yet at best, his ambiguous comparative evidence projects the argued differences more than it proves that either conjuncture necessarily produced rational capitalism, or, for that matter, that Protestantism was the main dynamic behind conjuncture!

Since his comparative procedures hardly and barely specify time and space (besides the elusive unit of 'civilizations' discussed), it is difficult to argue other than by rote assertion that within Western 'civilization' the noted three-factor conjuncture pre-supposing 'rational capitalism' necessarily happened where and when Protestantism became the dominant religious system. Weber slightly touches this latter issue in his comparison between England and France to depict the suggested correlation between Protestant-based (instrumental as opposed to Catholic value-rational based) ethical systems and industrialization, but the difference it claims to show by these examples does exude a strong scent of semantics.

While industrial capitalism may have made its debut in Protestant England, so did Catholic France eventually industrialize. So, does the fact that English industrialization preceded the French make the former more instrumentally rational than the latter variant? Or does the latter case rather show that indeed rational capitalism can emerge even in societies with per definition and according to Weber's own standards less instrumentally rational religious and ethical systems?

Moreover, when we stretch comparison (a point Weberian agenda suspiciously skirts) to some other Eastern cases (beyond China and India, where we do not find the outcome to be explained, i.e., industrial capitalism) like our proverbial Japan which contains a comparable outcome, then even more Weber's argument precariously wobbles. Here, we obtain a case of capitalist development not with but without Weber's prized dynamic Christian, let alone, Protestant-based economic ethos. With comparative omissions like this, Weber can make his arguments sound plausible just as easily as one doing the same, but this time eliding relevant Western cases with Protestant-based ethical systems, can make an alternative model of rational capitalism operated instead by, for example, a Buddhist or Confucian-based economic ethos, sound feasible.

In Skocpol's idiom thus, Weber's comparative procedure is designed primarily to bring out dramatic contrasts in order to illustrate, not test, his argument. But since the latter has causal explanatory claims, albeit contextual, those claims would without the benefit of testing, remain largely asserted; and such assertion, as we've seen, also easily haywires in the face of 'negative' cases like Japan.

Therborn's comparative empiricist agenda is an entirely different ball game. Here, you will find more open-ended empirical questions on different aspects of modernity rather than red thread interpretative arguments like Weber's, or testable hypothetical statements like Tilly's, or those of Skocpol's endeared macro-causal analytic agendas. It breaks down the modernity problem (Is modernity in the processes of structuration, spacing, enculturation and collective action/ steering still the rule?) into quantifiable variable-units, where comparative data (drawn from secondary cross-national statistical surveys in Western and Eastern Europe) are given more unconditional room to provide answers to empirical questions posed. If we are after potential anomalies it is therefore logical to search for them in the empirical procedures of this prominently empiricist agenda.

Firstly, a question triggered off by the dazzling amount of quantitative and qualitative data Therborn serves us is how actually comparable are they, and how reliable or representative are they (to what extent are they available) as operationalizing indicators of those modernity variables/ processes he singles out (structuration, enculturation, etc.)?

On the first count, the degree of comparability appears to vary with geography and across chosen variables. Statistical series available for EC and OECD countries are generally more comparable and continuous than those from Eastern Europe, while, some structuration variables lend themselves, for example, more easily to comparison than others (e.g., how to cope with prominently differing 'styles' of modern jurisprudence and law among European countries, or the nationally diverging distances between legal versus socially operative rights, if we are to assess modernity in terms of the structuration of rights to act), or they may be more comparable than, for instance, enculturation variables (i.e., cross-national data on identity, value-formation and time-perceptions).

On the second count, degree variations also seem to follow geography and variable designations: i.e., data on EC and OECD patterns are broadly more available and reliable than Eastern European as opposed to data on structuration patterns (means, tasks and rights), which are both more common and comprehensive than those for enculturation. There are, as Therborn notes, very few comprehensive European surveys on value patterns, and he draws enculturation data for Western countries basically from two such surveys—the 1986 Euro-barometer and the 1981/1990-91 World Value System Study. In contrast, no comparable surveys were available for Eastern Europe. Since value surveys used are of recent vintage, they provide data only for the past two decades, making, as such, analysis and appraisal of long-run changes in perception patterns problematic.

Above problem suggests that breaking the modernity concept down to measurable variables invites in turn assorted problems of measurability and measurement. Indeed, it is well advised to have them in mind in assaying the validity of the preliminary generalizations on the state of modernity Therborn draws from his empirical metrics.

Moving from hypothesis poor to rich and testing agendas, what gives in Tilly's claim-proof and comparative procedures? Taken together, his two works basically argue that war made states and revolutionary patterns followed the general sway of state development over time and space. Tilly test-runs the war-state and state-revolution halves of the equation through similar titanic comparative technics. For the first half of the equation to hold, Tilly has to empirically show that indeed there is such a correspondence—that war was the single most decisive function of most states, that the general changes in incidence, intensity, patterns of war-making co-varied with general changes in state structures over time and space— because the possibility that he might just be exaggerating the role of war a bit too much looms large.

As expected, in an agenda with Tilly's magnitude, data is a luxury item; and the little that may be available he moreover has to borrow from other historians. Thus, on the empirical frequency of wars, he depends on the generosity of Levy's data on number of wars involving the great powers from 1500-1900 suggesting a declining trend in the number, average duration and proportion for all years in which wars were in progress. However, the unaccounted remainder from 990-1500 is simply extrapolated in statements like, over the millennium as a whole, war has been the dominant activity of states in Europe. State budget, taxes and debts (i.e., indicators of the centrality of war as a function of state-making) reflect that reality (again, hardly any data to support the statement, except the cases of England and France), which, adds Tilly, arose from the late 1600s onwards to the rhythm of war (again no data, meaning, an assertion).

Rather than directing it to the hypothesized cause (war), he, in fact, spends the bulk of intensive comparative enterprise on the outcome he seeks to explain: the previous variety of state trajectories, later converging on a single national-state route with different variants. That effort Tilly devotes to testing, or, more precisely put, to illustrating a number of crucial sub-hypotheses: that the early multiplicity of state trajectories (capital, coercion-intensive, capitalized coercion) depended on varying capital-coercion ratios the secular level growth (accumulation and concentration) of which was conditioned in turn by the escalating exigencies of war (looping thus back to the main argument). Struggles for power positions in an increasingly denser inter-state system as a result of scaled-up war raised the stakes for state-building in general, in the context of which national states became the leading model over other forms because under given conditions only they were able to build effective war machineries to win those struggles.

Putting the stretch-shrink problems attached to the capital-coercion clockwork discussed earlier on, Tilly's comparative cases lend partial credence to noted hypotheses. The modifier, partial, should be emphasized because if one looks at the cases he discusses, taking his quantitative data on the number of states from 1490-1990 (200 commuting to a total of 25 plus states), no more than 8-10 cases of disparate state types are actually accounted for, and quite fleetingly at that (and in a way one loses temporal orientation).

With this in mind, we have here the makings of a general war-driven model of state development, nonetheless. Smith notes however that Tilly's war-state model may have to be reconsidered when we examine other cases like the US, where, if one discounts the mid-nineteenth century Civil War, the national federal state with all the celebrated features of Tilly's differentiated national states evolved not by virtue of war exigencies.

This brings us to the second half of the equation, where this time the state assumes the role of hypothesized cause and revolutions, the outcome to be explained. Like in the first half, Tilly has to empirically establish correspondence here as well; he does that through comparison, only now he performs it intensively throughout much of the book. The choice of cases stems from the previous capital-coercion ratio differences to illustrate correspondence between varying state trajectories, frequency and patterns of revolutionary situations and outcomes. While he sets the general time frame for all six cases to 1490-1990, he magnifies the comparative analysis one century in each to further dramatize, respectively, the parallelism between revolutionary peak and decline periods (he relies here as in the first half heavily on the chronologies of war and revolution by Levy) and periods of national state consolidation. Comparative findings seem to support cor-respondence. However, as in the first half, the same partiality clause would apply in this second half as well, considering the size of the samples used.

An earlier warning deserves reiteration. In some cases like the British Isles, it is sometimes technically problematic to distinguish inter-state wars from certain revolutionary situations/outcomes (e.g., civil war). For if we go back to the US example, the fact that national state consolidation followed after the resolution of the Civil War, and inter-state war (with Spain in the late 1890s; recall, Cuba, Puerto Rico and the Philippines) followed state consolidation, could very well be deployed to turn Tilly's equation around: that internal revolution made states and states made war!

Finally, we close with Zelizer. She goes against the grain of utilitarian market money models to ague that money is as powerful a solvent of social ties and personal exchange relations in some areas as it is powerfully constrained and recycled by social and cultural norms of exchange, in others. To highlight the workings of this dual process, particularly the latter, she looks at the comparative impact of expanding cash economy, consumerism and standardization of a single legal tender on three theoretically vulnerable social networks traditionally marked by relations of intimacy—household, gift-giving and charity—in the US between 1870-1930. She finds the persistence of multiple currencies and money earmarking in all three.

My immediate reflex reaction to her results is, why am I not that surprised? The correspondence of claim and proof makes automatic sense to me because I never really endorsed utilitarian assumptions (which Zelizer uses to justify her choice) that these three highly personalized networks should be that vulnerable to the corrosive powers of cash, precisely because of their prominently personal and informal character. It is thus reasonable to expect a significant degree of contes-tation and resistance to the overwhelmingly disruptive powers of cash once it enters these circuits, and as such one may reasonably anticipate Zelizer's findings.

Second, accepting her findings on face value, there is reason to weigh their 'currency-value' by asking from what data they were derived. Changing money earmarking processes were, judging from the main material, reconstructed from mostly qualitative secondary sources, specially etiquette, home-economics manual, some court proceedings and very few, mostly non-comprehensive quantitative national household surveys (some of them published in national magazines). Such findings might be excitingly illuminating, but they are logically largely anecdotal.

Thirdly, one wonders why she limited her time-frame to the 1930s. Had she pushed further into the 1960s, she would certainly have covered a period with strategic implications to her argument. She would have cut across the Depression, war mobilization and de-mobilization eras with their corollary effects not only on the ebb and flow of mass consumerist demand and commercialization, but also, as feminist scholarship informs us, on gender relations at home and work as well. How, for instance, was the process of earmarking affected by changing gender relations within the domestic sphere during these momentous intervals?

By stretching the time-frame, she could have made the case against utilitarian money theory perhaps even stronger, insofar as it was rather in the 1950s and 1960s than the early twentieth century that mass consumerism reached really epic proportions in the US and elsewhere. In this sense, finding similar patterns of social money earmarking could have doubled the lethal effect of her argument.

Fourthly, why not confront utilitarian theorists next time on their own market turfs and find out what different social networks and personalized ways of handling money, if any, arguably operated (where they theoretically are absolutely not supposed to) within market circuits. Within them, one may conceivably discover comparatively more subtle modes of earmarking than those found in Zelizer's relatively more impregnable networks.

6

CONCLUSION

TIMING THINK, THINKING TIME
WHAT'S WRONG WITH HISTORICAL SOCIOLOGY?

What defects intermittently appear in our amateur trouble-shooting notes on the four contrasting Historical Sociology agendas in the previous chapters? Our average short-list discloses two common sources of trouble printed on the verso of these agendas' advertised advantages: i.e., the application of concepts to history and the deployment of comparative technology in defense or illustration of the argument or questions raised. Common also to all is the fact that their comparative works almost always draw from secondary rather than primary sources and data produced by others.

Incidentally, upon consulting with more expert opinion from radical and reformist critics of Historical Sociology in a recent debate[32] we find our amateur premonitions confirmed.

---

[32]See ISSJ (1992), *op cit.*

In this dispute, we note the most uncompromising flak on Historical Sociology typically among puritan historians like Bertrand Badie who argues that history, seen as single events, is by nature resistant to analysis, let alone comparison. 'Macro-sociological disorder,' is, accordingly, 'too pronounced for there to be any hope of reconciling it with the rules of method' (a la Skocpol, if you like). He contends that the use of comparative analysis is tricky on account of different 'time scales' and historical periods involved. The variety of time conceptions across discrepant cultures (e.g., Western linear versus Islamic circular notions) makes it difficult to identify 'turning points.' Within circular time formats, for example, changes in history are not perceived as 'breaks' from one form to another, but more as a 'recombination' or 'redeployment.'

As historical sociologists commonly claim the comparability of histories and are prone to apply explanatory variables independent of the cultures associated with the subjects to be analyzed, then as Badie argues, they in effect interpret other histories by the code of one selected history.

Moreover, macro-sociological approach essentially contributes to the neglect of action in favor of 'system' and 'order.' Methodologically, its frequent use of multivariate analysis to draw causal relations can be specious because the variables developed are too heavy and composite (e.g., agrarian state/revolutions), and objects analyzed too extensive for operation to be meaningful.

A more reformist critical position is taken by historical sociologists such as Tilly (as he prefers to call himself). He flunks Badie on certain very arguable criticisms. One, is his point on the incomparability of histories due to the variability of time-scales and historical periods among cultures. Tilly's pain-killer to Badie's apprehensions: there is indeed structure and order in history in as much as:[33]

> "All social life is historical in two senses: we can only observe what has already happened, and what happened before strongly constrains what can happen now; social processes do not simply repeat themselves in the same sequences but are strongly path-dependent. That is why national trajectories are neither identical nor strictly comparable. Since all social life are historical however, its fundamental epistemological status is the same; the chief variations in what can be known of past and present result from the extensiveness of the residues of that social life available to contemporary observers, the extent to which new observations are possible to test inferences from the old, and the current familiarity of the codes in which the residues are embedded."

That is, rather than see social life as packaged in continuous 'societies' one should focus on processes, configurations, social relations, contingent connections and contexts. As an intermediate step, Tilly proposes to characterize eras and portions of the world by empirical delineation of dominant processes occurring in them and then frame testable propositions about the relation of other social changes to such dominant processes. Such a step would save one from having to wait for propositions that are true and tested in all historical times and places.

Historical uniformities show rather in the linkages between events, processes and structures. With this he suggests an alternative to heavy-weight structural approaches within Historical Sociology ranks, which incorrectly expected uniformities to take the shape of recurrent sequences.

Against Tilly's advice contra Badie's, that the proper unities for

---

[33]See ISSJ (1992), *op cit.*

comparison should be processes, events and structures rather than cultures, Leca, another reformist, argues nevertheless that one still has to ask how unities separated by blurred frontiers can be compared.

Whereas Hermet concludes that sociologists must approach history by getting rid of what he calls their 'repressed historian complex,' bringing us to our third noted shared weakness among historical sociologist—i.e., 'pushing beyond the collation of secondary accounts to the systematic analysis of primary historical materials ... so as not to compound the errors of the historians from whom they draw.'

This rookie tends to sympathize with Tilly's position and the added reminders of Hermet and Leca. Although taking Badie's critique seriously, there is no reason why one has to choose between the devil and the deep blue sea, so to speak. There are, as Tilly correctly notes, both structure/order and contingencies and disorder in history. The name of the game is to find the points where structure meets contingency. For if Badie is correct, I don't see any way for any culture to articulate his relativist time-conceptions in any intelligible manner or form; neither in structured language, symbols, nor signs! Regarding Hermet's repressed historian complex among historical sociologists, the latter has indeed a lot to learn from economic historians, many of whom seem to have overcome that kind of insecurity.

So after this long and tiresome day, the clockmaker can at last close shop and end with the note: there are unequivocally many roads and detours to Abrams' vision of 'making sociology tick, and history run clockwork.' The raw deal seems not to come down to any one-size-fits-all solution so much as to an omnivorous consumption of the best of both worlds, keeping in mind, as above critical forensic notes evinced, that comparability of units, the scale unit and timescale from and within which point any specific theoretical enquiry is to be addressed and plotted, do matter and may bear not insignificantly on the 'stretch and shrink-ability,' the elasticity if you like, of deployed theoretical concepts!

APPENDIX

Figure 1
Basic phases & format of Smith's map of postwar Historical Sociology (HS)

	Phase I (1950-60s)	Phase II (1960-70s)	Phase III (1970-80s)
Politics/Ideology in command	Liberal democracy expounded	Liberal democracy exposed	Capitalism explored and exposed
HS status/position	Strategic defensive	Strategic offensive	Strategic offensive
HS format			
Big think problem focus	System-integration/stability/consensus	Systems contradictions/ power/ domination/ inequality/ resistance	Multiple modes of production, capitalist world system, relative autonomy of system of power & domination
Big time (history-theory ratio)	Low>High	Higher	Higher
Comparison -case density -unit/character -use-mode	-single>multiple -nation-state -theory-demonstration	-single<multiple -nation-state -theory-testing, interpretative, analytic	-single<multiple -nation-state/world system -theory-testing, interpretative, analytic
HS case sample (n)	6	6	7
-trend-setters	-Parsons. Smelser, Lipset, Eisenstadt	-Moore, Thompson	-Wallerstein, Anderson, Skocpol, Tilly, Braudel, Mann, Giddens
-trend-breakers	-Marshall, Bendix	-Lenski, Runciman, Bloch, Elias	

PHOTO-MONTAGE: OUR INTERLOCUTORS

Charles Tilly
1929-2008

Max Weber (to the right of Kafka)
1864-1920

Göran Therborn, 1941- (top), Theda Skocpol, 1947 (bottom)

Viviana Zelizer, 1946-

REFERENCES

Abrams, Philip (1982) *Historical Sociology*. London: Open Books.

Anderson, Perry (1974) *Passages from Antiquity to Feudalism*. London: New Left Books.

— (1974) *Lineages of the Absolutist State*. London: New Left Books.

Bakhtin, M.M. (1981) T*he Dialogic Imagination: Four Essays*. Ed. Michael Holquist. trans. Caryl Emerson and Michael Holquist. Austin and London: University of Texas Press.

— (1993) *Towards a Philosophy of the Act*. Austin: University of Texas Press.

Bellah, Robert N (1970) *Tokugawa Religion: The Values of Pre-Industrial Japan*. Boston: Beacon Press.

Bendix, Reinhard (1960) *Max Weber: An Intellectual Portrait*. NY: Doubleday Anchor.

— (1974) *Work and Authority in Industry*. Berkeley: UCP.

Bloch, Marc (1966) *French Rural History: An Essay on Its Basic Characteristics*, trans. Janet Sondheimer. London: Routledge & Kegan Paul.

Block, Fred (1977) T*he Origins of International Economic Disorder:*

A Study of United States International Monetary Policy From World War II to the Present. Berkeley: UCP.

— (1987) *Revising State Theory: Essays in Politics and Post-Industrialism.* Philadelphia: Temple University Press.

— (1990) *Post-Industrial Possibilities: A Critique of Economic Discourse.* Berkeley: UCP.

— (1997) *The Vampire State: And Other Myths and Fallacies About the US Economy.* New York: The New Press.

— & Somers, Margaret R (2014) *The Power of Market Fundamentalism: Karl Polanyi's Critique.* Cambridge, MA: Harvard University Press.

Braudel, Fernand, trans. Sian Reynolds (1966) *The Mediterranean World in the Age of Philip II, Vol. 1.* Berkeley: UCP.

— (1966) *The Mediterranean World in the Age of Philip II, Vol. 2.* NY: Harper Collins.

— (1967) *Civilization and Capitalism 15th-18th Century, Vol. 1: The structure of everyday life.* Berkeley: UCP.

— (1979) *Civilization and Capitalism 15th-18th Century, Vol. 2: The wheels of commerce.* Berkeley: UCP.

— (1979) (1967) *Civilization and Capitalism 15th-18th Century, Vol. 3: The perspective of the world.* Berkeley: UCP.

Chirot, Daniel (1976) *Social Change in a Peripheral Society: Creation of a Balkan Colony (Studies in social discontinuity).* Academic Press Inc.

— (1977) *Social Change in the Twentieth Century.* San Diego: Harcourt College Pub.

Coronel, S (1995) "Cavite: The Killing Fields of Commerce," in Lacaba J ed *Boss: 5 Case Studies of Local Politics in the Philippines.*

Manila: IPD.

Eisenstadt S N (1969) *Political Systems of Empires*. Collier Macmillan Ltd.

Fulbrook, Mary (1992) *The Divided Nation: A History of Germany, 1918-1990*. New York: Oxford University Press.

Giddens, Anthony (1971) *Capitalism and Modern Social Theory*. Cambridge: CUP.

Hamilton, Gary, Orru M & NW Boggart (1996) *The Economic Organization of East Asian Capitalism*. London: Sage Publications.

Hermet, Guy (1992) "On Historical Obstinacy." *ISSJ* 133: 343-350.

Hunt, Lynn A (1978) *Revolution and Urban Politics in Provincial France: Troyes and Reims, 1786-1790*. Redwood City: Stanford University Press.

— (1984) *Politics, Culture, and Class in the French Revolution*. Berkeley: UCP.

Irschick, Eugene (1994) *Dialogue and History: Constructing South India, 1795-1895*. Berkeley: UCP.

Kennedy, Paul (1987) *The Rise and Fall of the Great Powers. Economic Change and Military Conflict from 1500-2000*. New York: Vintage Books.

Kohli A, Evans P, Przeworski A, Katzenstein P, Scott J and Skocpol T (1995) "The Role of Theory in Comparative Politics: A Symposium." *World Politics* Vol 48 (October): 1-49.

Leca, Jean (1992) "Post-Face: Has Historical Sociology Gone Back to its Infancy? Or When Sociology Gave Up to History," *ISSJ* 133: 403-415.

Lipset, Seymour M (1950) *Agrarian Socialism*. Berkeley: UCP.

McMichael, Philip (1992) "Rethinking Comparative Analysis in a Post-Development Context," *ISSJ* 133: 351-366.

Mills, C Wright (1959) *The Sociological Imagination*. New York: OUP.

Moore Jr, Barrington (1966) *Social Origins of Dictatorship and Democracy: Lord and Peasant in the Making of the Modern World*. Boston: Beacon Press.

Parsons, Talcott (1951) *The Social System*. Glencoe, Ill: Free Press.

— (1966) *Societies: Evolutionary & Comparative Perspectives*. NJ: Prentice-Hall.

Polanyi, Karl (1944, 1957) *The Great Transformation: The Political and Economic Origins of Our Time*. Boston: Beacon Press by arrangement with Rinehart & Company, Inc.

—, Conrad M. Arensberg & Harry W. Pearson. (1957) *Trade and Market in the Early Empires: Economies in History and Theory*. Glencoe, Illinois: The Free Press.

Ragin, Charles (1987) *The Comparative Method: Moving Beyond Qualitative and Quantitative Strategies*. Berkeley, LA, London: UCP.

— (1994) *Constructing Social Research: The Unity and Diversity of Method*. Newbury Park: Pine Forge Press.

Reuschemeyer, Dietrich (1986) *Power and the Division of Labor*. Redwood City: Stanford University Press.

— Stephens JD & Stephens EH (1992) *Capitalist Development and Democracy*. Chicago: University of Chicago Press.

Rojas, Virgilio (1997) "Making Sociology Tick and History Run Clockwork: Project, Prospects and Problems of 'Big Think' and 'Big Time.'" Dept. of Economic History, Stockholm University.

Runciman, WG (1969) *Social Science & Political Theory*.

Cambridge: CUP.

— (1970) *Sociology in its Place & Other Essays*. Cambridge: CUP.

Schama, Simon (1987) *The Embarrassment of Riches: An Interpretation of Dutch Culture in the Golden Age*. Collins.

Skocpol, Theda (1984) *Vision and Method in Historical Sociology*. New York: CUP.

Smelser, Neil J & Warner, Stephen R (1976) *Sociological Theory: Historical & Formal*. Morristown, NJ: General Learning Press.

Smith, Dennis (1991) *The Rise of Historical Sociology*. Cambridge: Polity Press.

Somers, Margaret R (2008) *Genealogies of Citizenship: Markets, Statelessness and the Right to Have Rights*. Cambridge, MA: Cambridge University Press.

Therborn, Göran (1995) *European Modernity and Beyond: The Trajectory of European Societies, 1945-2000*. London: Sage.

Thompson, EP (1966) *The Making of the English Working Class*. New York: Vintage/Alfred A Knopt/Random House.

Tilly, Charles (1993) *European Revolutions, 1492-1992*. Oxford: Blackwell.

—(1990) *Coercion, Capital and European States, AD 990-1992*. Oxford: Blackwell.

Trimberger Ellen Kay (1978) *Revolution from Above: Military Bureaucrats and Development in Japan, Turkey, Egypt, and Peru*. New Jersey: Transaction Books.

Wallerstein, Immanuel (1974) *The Modern World-System: Capitalist Agriculture & the Origins of the European World-Economy in the Sixteenth Century*. NY: Academic Press.

Weber, Max (1986) *Kapitalismens Uppkomst* (med urval och förord av Hans Zetterberg) Göteborg: Timbro AB.

Zelizer, Vivian (1994) *The Social Meaning of Money*. New York: Basic Book.

INDEX

Durkheim, E 10, 16, 20, 23-24

dynastic revolutions 48-52

E

economic spirit/ethos 27-29, 31, 38, 75

Eisenstadt, SN 8, 10-11, 15, 20, 23-24, 91

Elias, N 11, 13, 91

enculturation 33, 69

England 29, 39, 50, 74-75, 78

epoch 28-29, 32, 38, 64, 68, 71

era of nationalization 41

European revolutions 44-53

Evans, P 8

F

France 21-22, 29, 39, 50-51, 74-75

Fullbrook, Mary 15

G

Genoa 44

gestalt 62

Giddens, A 11, 14

H

Habermas 53

Hamilton, Gary 16

Hermet, Guy 5, 8, 86

Hinduism 30

History 1-4, 6. 8, 10-12, 16, 24

Historical Sociology

def 1-8

Hungary 39, 44, 49

I

Iberia 49-50, 72

instrumental rationality 27-28, 33, 54, 60, 68, 73

India 28-29, 30

Indian karma-thought 30

institution

charity 55-57

family 53, 55-56

gift-giving 56-57

inter-state system 43-44

inter-state wars 43, 80

Islam 30

JK

Japan 32, 65

Katzenstein, P 8

Kennedy, Paul 14

Kohli, A 8

L

Leca, Jean 3, 5, 8, 86

ABOUT THE AUTHOR

Virgilio Rojas (*b* 1957, *pob* Manila, Philippines) took undergraduate and graduate studies in Economic History at the Department of Economic History at the University of Stockholm in the late 80s—early 90s and between 1998-2004. He was research assistant at the Seminar for Development Studies, Department of Government at the University of Uppsala between 1993-1997. He was technical editor of the book *Democratization in the Third World: Concrete Cases in Comparative and Theoretical Perspective*, co-edited by Professors Lars Rudebeck and Olle Törnqvist and published by Macmillan Press Ltd. in London in 1996 & 1998.

He was awarded research grants by the University-stewarded Kinanders Foundation for three consecutive years between 2001-2004 and the Swedish Agency for Research Cooperation (SAREC) in 1998. He taught and supervised undergraduate & monographic courses in "Global Economic History" and "Transnational Organized Crime" at the Department of Economic History, Stockholm University between 1998-2004. A few of his academic works in the themes of Gender & Work, Historical Sociology, Latin American Economic History, Criminal and Colonial History, Social Movements, Post-Colonial Urban History, Collective Alienation and Action, are now available and down-loadable for free at Scribd.com/siokoyr and https://su-se.academia.edu-/VirgilioRojas.

Currently, he works for the City Government of Stockholm in the field of Social Psychiatry.